KT-424-070

CHILDREN AND COMMUNITIES

Edited by
Paul Henderson

The Children's Society

COMMUNITY
DEVELOPMENT
FOUNDATION

P L U T O   P R E S S

First published 1995 by Pluto Press
345 Archway Road, London N6 5AA
and 5500 Central Avenue
Boulder, Colorado 80301, USA
in association with
Community Development Foundation
60 Highbury Grove
London N5 2AG
Registered Charity No. 306130
and
The Children's Society
Edward Rudolph House
69–85 Margery Street
London WC1X 0JL
Registered Charity No. 221124

British Library Cataloguing in Publication Data
A catalogue record for this book is available from
the British Library

ISBN 0 7453 0798 1 hb

Library of Congress Cataloging in Publication Data
is available from the Library of Congress

98   97   96   95
 4   3   2   1

Designed and produced for Pluto Press by
Chase Production Services, Chipping Norton, OX7 5QR
Typeset from CDF disks by Stanford DTP Services
Printed in the EC by TJ Press

Contents

Contributors

Roger Adams is an internal consultant working for The Children's Society.

Katy Green has worked in play, youth and community work throughout Leicestershire, and ran the Street Play Project as an Assistant Director for the National Children's Play and Recreation Unit. She now works partly in community consultation, and partly in film and video work with young people.

Ruth Hall helped to establish West Leeds FSU and was its first Unit Organiser until 1993 when she moved to CCETSW as an Adviser and Development Officer (Child Care). Her experience in the last 15 years spans staff development, management, and consultancy, mainly in the voluntary sector, working with children and families in community-based projects.

Joe Hasler is an Anglican priest working in the outer estate parish of Hartcliffe, Bristol. Previously a community development worker, for 15 years he worked in Birmingham, Essex, Liverpool and Bristol. Much of that time he worked for The Children's Society with an interest in the part children play in community life.

Paul Henderson is Director, North of England and Scotland, at the Community Development Foundation. He has been closely involved with community development for more than 20 years, initially as a practitioner and trainer, and more recently as a consultant and manager. He has written extensively on the theory and practice of community work and community practice.

Rachel Hodgkin was a founder member and then worked in the Children's Legal Centre. Previously, she worked in a community law centre. She is currently Principal Policy Officer at the National Children's Bureau.

Peter Newell is co-ordinator of the campaign EPOCH – End Physical Punishment of Children, and Chair of the Council of the Children's Rights Development Unit.

Sarah O'Grady has been a social worker for 12 years. She has worked with children and families in community and social work settings. She is currently a Guardian-ad Litem in Humberside.

Dr Rupert Prime has had experience as a headteacher of comprehensive schools in inner London and has been a magistrate for 20 years. He was until recently a member of the Board of Governors of the University of the South Bank of which he is an Honorary Fellow.

Jim Radford, a campaigning community worker for 30 years, has worked for Blackfriars Settlement, Manchester CVS, the Community Resource Unit and Ealing Unified Community Action.

Craig Russell has been a community development worker in inner city Manchester for the last ten years. He is currently working for the Salford Urban Mission Training Programme. He is a member of the United People's Church, Moss Side.

Theresa Smith teaches about community work and preschool policy in the Department of Applied Social Studies and Social Research in the University of Oxford. She has recently completed a research study of family centres.

Community Development Foundation

Community Development Foundation (CDF) was set up in 1968 to pioneer new forms of community development. The Community Development Foundation's mission is to strengthen communities by ensuring the effective participation of people in determining the conditions which affect their lives. CDF does this through:

- providing support for community initiatives
- promoting best practice
- informing policy-makers at local and national level.

As a leading authority on community development in the UK and Europe, CDF is a non-departmental public body and receives support from the Voluntary Services Unit of the Home Office. It receives substantial backing from local and central government, trusts and business.

CDF promotes community development by enabling people to work in partnership with public authorities, government, business and voluntary organisations to regenerate their communities through:

- local action projects
- conferences and seminars
- consultancies and training programmes
- research and evaluation services
- parliamentary and public policy analysis
- information services
- CDF News, a quarterly newsletter
- publications.

Chairman: Alan Haselhurst, MP
Chief Executive: Alison West

Community Development Foundation
60 Highbury Grove
London N5 2AG
Tel: 071 226 5375
Fax: 071 704 0313
Registered Charity No: 306130

The Children's Society

The Children's Society is a Christian organisation which exists to work for children and young people:

- to help them grow in their families and communities
- to help them take charge of their own lives
- to help them change the conditions which stand in their way.

The Children's Society runs more than 120 projects throughout England and Wales including:

- family centres and neighbourhood groups in local communities where families are under stress often feeling isolated and powerless to improve their lives
- working with young people living on the street
- promoting children's and young people's rights
- residential and day care for young people's rights
- providing independent living units for young people leaving care
- helping children and young people with special needs to find new families.

The Children's Society is also committed to raising public awareness of issues affecting children and young people and to promoting the welfare and rights of children and young people in matters of public policy. It produces a range of publications, including reports, briefing papers, and educational material.

For further information please contact:

The Children's Society
Edward Rudolf House
Margery Street
London WC1X 0JL
Tel: 071 837 4299

Foreword

Penelope Leach Ph.D., C.Psychol., FBPsS.

Childhood and community are such familiar concepts in contemporary discussions of social issues that our ignorance of children's experience or sense of community has gone unnoticed. We are all indebted to the Community Development Foundation and the Children's Society, supported by the Calouste Gulbenkian Foundation, for drawing attention to it and opening up the search for a better understanding of how children relate to their neighbourhoods and of the factors that encourage a sense of relatedness.

The essays in this book are biased toward practical experience and provide an important opportunity for professionals to describe and reflect upon work in many different fields. But out of their diversity one consistent message emerges: community is not only where we live and who we live with – our neighbourhood and neighbours – but also how we shape and are shaped by that place and those people: our power and our participation. Children, even more than adults, often lack both.

Children and Communities contains key points that I hope will both stimulate and guide policymakers and practitioners. There is an overall and overriding need for programmes that empower children's participation. Successful programmes need to engage with the many different ways in which children experience 'community', to understand not only the issues which children face, but the complex linkages between them and therefore to be coordinated one with another. Even then, the programmes that truly empower children will not just be set up in such a way that children are genuinely able to participate, but set up that way enthusiastically, because children's capacity to act creatively and constructively is trusted and welcomed.

Although this book is a rich source of ideas for all those who work, or facilitate work, with children, it contains no blueprints for easy action; no programmes waiting for replication. Reading *Children and Communities* reinforces my conviction that if there is to be effective action for children at local level, government must address child poverty at national level. The statistics and experiences gathered here tell us about poor children in poor neighbourhoods. They tell us that for many children participation means being involved in the collective struggles of their neighbours to achieve dignity, self respect and a decent standard of living.

It is government's responsibility to facilitate better economic conditions, education and opportunities for children, but a government that did all that would not have discharged, but merely laid the foundations for, its responsibilities towards children. Under the UN Convention on the Rights of the Child, governments are committed to prioritising children's needs and children's rights: to moving towards the child-friendly society that it is the individual responsibility of every one of us to build.

The Calouste Gulbenkian Foundation has actively supported work on children's rights for many years, including the case for a statutory Children's Commissioner, and setting up a Commission on Children and Violence. *Children and Communities* calls for children's right to participate to be rigorously applied in the context of neighbourhood.

A child-friendly UK is difficult to imagine because, as the conclusion to *Children and Communities* points out, 'as a society our sentimentality over children runs little more than skin-deep ...' and 'In the UK there is no serious sign of good intentions.' We cannot act for what we cannot even imagine, so this final chapter helps us to see something of what a child-friendly family or school, neighbourhood, or nation might be like and to see the need for individual commitment for that vision, 'Until children's rights are given reality in the home, and in neighbourhoods and communities by action they remain abstract ... Moving on from where we are now demands mechanisms for moving from the abstract into practice, and schools, projects and local initiatives can provide many of them ...'

May *Children and Communities* and the projects and practices described in it serve to move us all on.

Preface

Children's rights or children's needs? This question runs through all the contributions to *Children and Communities*: a rights-based approach to working with children appears often to be in tension with a needs-based approach. They exist alongside each other, only occasionally complementing each other.

Rights have the advantage of being specific, and can be upheld by law. Needs, on the other hand, can be vague and are more open to challenge. Community development usually operates within the latter framework, and one conclusion which can be drawn from the contributions in this book is that there are advantages to be gained from linking children's needs to children's rights.

One of the strengths of community development is to ask the awkward questions and to point out things which are missing. This happens here. The experience of compiling the book has been to reveal our lack of knowledge of the extent and type of community activities which are genuinely children-led. We are adults looking into the world of children – and this in itself raises many questions. But we are also adults who are surprisingly ignorant about the capacity of children to initiate and determine positive and creative activities in communities without adult involvement being dominant.

The editorial group from the Community Development Foundation, the Gulbenkian Foundation and the Children's Society were not fully aware of this issue when they began planning the book. At the forefront of our minds was a concern to bring together ideas and practical examples which would re-assert the fundamental importance of 'community' for children, and how community development has the potential to help make connections between communities and children. The book, in my opinion, does this. It also raises serious questions about the practice of community-based work with children and the policies which have such a profound impact on practice. What it does not do is provide a blueprint of children-led activities. That is for the future.

Children and Communities offers the specialist reader a broader perspective. It is a generalist, multi-disciplinary contribution to the discussion of children, neighbourhoods and communities. It aims to identify and analyse themes and issues which are common to more than one discipline, and to give these value. Thus, while the book's structure allows the reader to select a particular focus of work with children, the purpose is to understand the chapters 'in the round', to make connections between disciplines and to see how it is as a totality that they relate to children's lives in communities.

Our memories of childhood and communities tend to be powerful and evocative. They consist of interlinking layers of reality and imagination and they are influenced, sometimes determined, by events and changing social structures. I was born in Oxfordshire, brought up in London and have spent most of my working life in Yorkshire. What does this make me? What connections with neighbourhoods and other children have I taken with me from childhood to adult life?

A similar mix of experiences is apparent in the way the contributors write about their memories and understanding of childhood, and hence their perceptions of children today. This connection between personal experiences and professional opinion can be identified in both kinds of chapter which will be found in each part of the book: the chapters which are capturing examples of practice and making sense of them, and the chapters which address policy questions.

In the Introduction I set out the central ideas which have informed the book's evolution, while at the same time raising questions about the gaps and weaknesses in how professionals and their agencies work with children in communities.

Part One begins with two practice examples relating to the theme of care and protection of children. Roger Barford, Sarah O'Grady and Ruth Hall write about the work undertaken with children by West Leeds Family Service Unit and Kanchan Jadeja uses examples from Leicester to address the issues of black children in care. Then Teresa Smith examines some of the policy questions which are central to care and protection, especially the Children Act 1989.

The theme of children and the environment is becoming increasingly important. In Part Two we include a detailed case study

by Katy Green of traffic calming as it relates to children's safety
and play in part of Leicester, and a more wide-ranging discussion
by Jim Radford of how children can become involved in environmental issues in both community and school settings.

Part Three opens up the critical areas of educational experiences
in relation to communities. Rupert Prime tells the story of how
a London school developed links with community resources,
whereas Rachel Hodgkin examines the theme of 'community'
within the school setting.

Part Four is concerned with the relationship of children to
neighbourhoods. Craig Russell provides an insight into the lives
and action of children and adults in Manchester's Moss Side and
Hulme, Roger Adams uses a case study of children's play and theatre
in a London neighbourhood to develop the theme of children's
need for place identity, while Joe Hasler draws upon his community
work experience to discuss how children can be helped, in the
neighbourhood setting, both to belong to networks and to develop
as individuals.

In the final chapter Peter Newell brings us back to children's
rights, challenging us to see how different the world would be if
a range of rights were taken seriously. He also demonstrates the
inseparability of participation and neighbourhood from the
struggle for rights. He outlines an agenda for change while at the
same time acknowledging the advances which have been achieved.
While referring to key points arising from other contributors'
chapters, his conclusions in a sense take the reader back to
questions raised in the introductory chapter.

Acknowledgements

Children and Communities was produced with the help of the UK
Branch of the Calouste Gulbenkian Foundation and in collabo-
ration with The Children's Society. Paul Curno at the Gulbenkian
Foundation gave support and encouragement to the project from
beginning to end. I am grateful to him, and to the other members
of the book's advisory group: Roger Smith of the Children's
Society, Peter Newell of EPOCH and David Thomas, the previous
Chief Executive of CDF. I would particularly like to thank Penelope
Leach for finding the time to write the Foreword.

In the course of agreeing with contributors the focus of their
chapters I came into contact with a wide range of individuals and

organisations – too many to list. My thanks go to them and to the contributors for extending my knowledge and vision. The contributors responded readily to my requests and deadlines and I am deeply indebted to them for their commitment and insights.

The book's progress owed a great deal to the guidance of Catriona May (CDF's Head of Publications), Pluto Press, and Ann Nicholls in CDF's Leeds office, to the forebearance of colleagues for taking the strain at critical points in the making of the book, and to the support of CDF's present Chief Executive, Alison West, and her Trustees.

I was always aware of the ultimate irony: the danger that the book's demands would erode time with my own children. They and my wife must be the judges of that, but of the strength of their support I have no doubt at all.

Paul Henderson,
October 1994

Introduction: Context and Rationale

Paul Henderson

The theme of children and communities begs many questions. In one sense, all children belong to communities which are easily recognisable: their schools, clubs, friends and the neighbourhoods in which they live. Yet this 'catch-all' sense of community tends to reinforce a broad, inexact use of the term. Indeed, the willingness to go along with this convention may help to explain why the community dimension of children's lives has received such scant treatment by policy makers, experts and researchers compared with the research outputs arising from particular perspectives – child care, child psychology, child psychiatry, early education, etc.

A working definition of 'community' is needed. I have sought to give it

- a strong sense of place or neighbourhood
- a definite meaning of shared identity – the 'community of children'. Community is therefore defined as meaning both locality and children's worlds.

Both these ingredients of community allow for the scope and imagination of children, for them to define their communities. Readers will find that the contributions move between these two 'pillars' of community – the neighbourhoods where children live and 'community' as belonging to children's thoughts and values. The element common to both of them is the involvement of children and/or adults in creating 'community'. It cannot be constructed outside their experiences.

There is an additional problem facing those who work with and write about children, namely the confusing juxtaposition of popular assumptions and views held about children. These range

1

from the view of children as representing naturalness, purity and beauty to the view of children as beings who possess innate cruelty and selfishness. Marina Warner, in drawing attention to the separation that has taken place between the worlds of children and adults, comments that 'never before have children been so saturated with all the power of projected monstrousness to excite repulsion – even terror' (Warner, 1994). These perceptions can be traced through time as well as within and across cultures. Pervading much of this cultural and social 'heritage' is a strong element of adult sentimentality towards children and a failure by adults to address the issues of power as it relates to their relationship with children. The competing perceptions are powerful and emotive and act as a screen through which it can be difficult to question existing orthodoxies. The experiences and actions of adults also impact directly on children, a point made by Marina Warner:

> Much has been done over the last ten years to make life hard for parents – and for parents, read above all, mothers. And everything that makes life hard for parents makes it harder for children. In the era of the market force child, children are suffering, and with them, all of us are being damaged. (Warner, 1989)

In this introduction I propose to open up the theme of children and communities by providing an overall context. I will also discuss three ideas which underpin the chapters which follow:

- children and participation
- children and neighbourhoods
- the relationship between the practice of working with children and the policies which shape practice.

It is hoped that this 'rationale' will highlight the fundamental importance of the theme of children and community and will go some way towards countering criticism that the approach is unacceptably broad and general.

Context

Facts which show the injustices and suffering experienced by children are well known: three million children in Britain live in poverty; only 9 per cent of 7 to 10 year olds were allowed to go to school on their own in 1990 compared with 80 per cent in 1971; children on deprived council estates are more likely to suffer injury and death than children living in wealthy areas; evidence suggests that pollutants such as ozone and sulphur dioxide can trigger and aggravate children's asthma; since the death of Maria Colwell in 1973 there have been over 40 similar investigations into child death, injury or abuse. And so on.

It is rare, however, to have an analysis which puts together the pieces of the jigsaw, which presents the various categories of data as a whole. This has two effects: first, we tend to try to understand children through an array of professional and academic perspectives, each one of which is of immense significance in its own right but only some of which become linked – western culture does not see the whole child, it does not see the child as part of the community; second, we tend to remain trapped within the framework of 'the child', essentially an individualistic concept, rather than think about the broader notion of childhood.

'Sectorisation' of Children's Services

The organisation of children's services and facilities has generally had the effect of reinforcing a 'sectorised' approach to working with children. Within each of the following professions there is evidence of real engagement with the community aspects of children's lives. What is questionable is if connections have been made, from a community perspective, *between* issues and if the potential *within* each profession to develop a community dimension has been realised.

Social Work

The history of child welfare undoubtedly offers a rich and varied display of initiatives and programmes aimed at providing services for children within a community or neighbourhood context. These are explored by Heaton and Sayer (1992) and discussed by Teresa Smith in this volume.

There is an important legislative aspect to the debate. In principal the Children Act 1989, because of its emphasis on prevention and providing support for families in need, offers major opportunities for social services departments to rediscover the community focused origins of social work. Yet over the last 15 years it has been within the voluntary sector that innovatory approaches in this area have, in the main, been tried. Nowhere has this been more evident than within the development of family centres, especially those – such as the centre described in Part 1 – which have taken a strong neighbourhood focus. Such centres are located firmly within the context of prevention and family support measures. Research by Gibbons (1990) leads her to state that family projects had 'strengthened local community resources, by providing new activities and advice points, by drawing in new volunteers, and by opening up new opportunities for local people' (p. 158).

Education

'Community' has been of major, if inconsistent, concern to all parts of the education system. For example, it received rigorous treatment in the Educational Priority Area projects of the late 1960s, and community service by schoolchildren and the issue of parental involvement in schools have been recurrent themes. The extent to which pupils themselves have organised collectively in this country is another important aspect of 'community' and education (Adams, 1991).

However, it has been adult and community education, notably through outreach work and by encouraging schools and centres to be used as resources for the community, which have engaged most powerfully with community strategies and methods. Thomas (1983) has shown that the education sector failed to build upon its community development experience, even compared with social work. The combination, in the 1980s, of public expenditure cuts and major changes in the organisation and funding of education has resulted in the decline of most community programmes of schools and local education authorities. The introduction of the National Curriculum at the end of the 1980s has had the effect of reducing further the integration of school and community because of teachers' lack of time. Only in Scotland, where there is a strong tradition of adult education, is there evidence of a commitment to maintaining community education and informal adult education.

Play

The capacity of play – pre-school playgroups, after-school clubs, adventure playgrounds, playschemes – to respond to children's needs and interests is clear. Play can release and channel the energies of children in ways which counter the falterings of even the most hard-bitten practitioner. In recent years, energy has been put into developing a Charter for Play. There have also been local campaigns arguing for a comprehensive approach to play. Leeds Play Network, for example, states that, 'the local authority, the voluntary sector and schools should collaborate in order to establish suitable provision of play in the community', and highlights the 'non-use phenomenon' in neighbourhood parks. Planners are becoming increasingly aware of the extent to which play can develop in streets, squares and parking lots (Guichard and Ader, 1991), a trend supported by Roger Adams in his chapter below.

Playschemes are often linked to community arts, and the combination can produce highly imaginative events which succeed in engaging with real community issues in addition to providing space and resources for children to enjoy and to find out about themselves (see Clinton and Glen, 1993).

Frequently, local people commit themselves to these activities in the face of considerable obstacles – non-existent or weak play policies of local authorities, poor sites, and dwindling grants.

Environment
The growing awareness of environmental issues among children, which is discussed by Jim Radford in his chapter, is relatively recent, and it will be important to observe the extent and form of commitment over the next few years. The experience of support agencies, such as the Newcastle Architectural Workshop, of working on environmental issues with community groups is that engaging with the hopes and aspirations of children is crucial. Their future is at stake. Furthermore, they may be in a better position than adults to see the necessity for sharing – self-interest not selfishness must be a key building block of sustainable development. We need to remember how adults are often either indifferent or hostile to children; researchers working on the report *Out of Hours*, a study of social and cultural life in 12 town centres, were often asked, 'Do the British actually like children?', in response to the observation that families were rarely to be seen on British streets at night compared with many other cities in the world (Comedia, 1991).

While not wishing to exaggerate the 'demarcations' between these four professions and issues, as well as others, the absence of overall strategies which deliberately seek to link together a range of programmes around the themes of 'community' or community development is striking. Policy makers and managers in agencies concerned in different ways with children's needs appear to have shied away from the issue of community involvement; if it happens, and if it works, all well and good, but it remains subservient to other concerns. Resources to support it have, in general, been meagre.

The issue of prisoners' children is an example of children being made dispensable; Roger Shaw (1989) refers to 'a conspiracy of silence because the criminal justice system must sacrifice these children, must permit them to become its victims if it is not to question its basis'. Children as carers of elderly and disabled people (Aldridge and Becker, 1993) is a further example of how groups of children are excluded from opportunities to participate in community life.

Community Development
Even within community development itself, the question of how to work effectively with children, with the aim of encouraging action by children themselves, has often been secondary to other community development goals. Making contact with children and their parents has frequently been used by community workers as a means to an end rather than as an end in its own right – an issue explored by Joe Hasler in his chapter. As an inexperienced, isolated community worker wondering how to gain entry to the culture and networks of a small Yorkshire mining town, I remain indebted to the primary school head who helped me meet mothers and set up a community playgroup. My ultimate aim, however, was to work with adults on housing and community care issues.

If there have been examples of 'children-led' community development, they have not in the main been written up so that others can learn from them. There has also been a reluctance to build upon pilot projects and research. For example, the experience in the early 1970s of the Harlesden Project (Harlesden Community Project, 1979), which deliberately set out to make connections between community work practice and caring for children in an inner-city area, does not appear to have been picked up elsewhere by community workers and social workers.

More serious has been the failure of community development to make the connections between children, poverty and unemployment: children in poor communities who are without possessions, places and participation; and children whose lives are blighted as a result of the long-term unemployment of their parents and neighbours. A co-ordinator of the Castleford Women's

Centre in Yorkshire speaks in the following terms about the lives of children in decimated coalfield communities:

> Our children where we are don't even know how to talk to other children because they're at home with their mums all day, their mums are depressed, they won't go out and therefore they're not meeting anybody. The children come to our centres and they don't know how to talk to other people. (Barbara Smith, 1993, p. 101)

Practitioners have yet to respond to this challenge with a practice theory which values children's thoughts and experiences in their own right.

Equally surprising has been the sluggish response by policy makers to community-based child development programmes in Britain and the United States, some of which have demonstrated positive gains for children. Wood (1991) has argued that 'early childhood programmes which rest within the framework of community mobilisation can be essential instruments in opening the way to much more widespread community change'.

It should be recalled that the national Community Development Projects (CDP) (1968–77) had their origin in the Home Office in changes in the law on children and young persons. Mayo (1975) notes that these proposals related to similar proposals for a 'more rational, more co-ordinated and more family and community based approach to individuals and families in trouble' (p. 7). CDP took a radical change of direction, but why did community workers and others not come back to the original issue?

One explanation for community workers' reluctance to place children at the centre of their projects and strategies is that put forward by Baldock (1983) about community care: compared with the 'hard' issues of housing and unemployment, work with so-called client groups – children, elderly people and people with mental illnesses – have often been perceived as 'soft', as well as too closely aligned with social control. A more generous explanation is that community workers have been genuinely baffled as to how to make children the central focal point: how can they help children to do things for themselves when so many forces from the opposite direction impact on children, telling them what to do and what to buy?

Some of the child care voluntary organisations have sought to broaden the perspectives of agencies. Roger Smith, writing about putting rights into practice, gives the example of excessive traffic in local streets being a critical factor affecting children's rights to associate freely and to play (articles 15 and 31 of the UN Convention on the Rights of the Child (1989)):

> This example is chosen deliberately because it helps to demonstrate firstly how widespread are the implications of a comprehensive concern for the development and protection of children's rights; and secondly, how concern for specific rights has a direct bearing on the lives of children in communities. (Smith, 1992)

Children, in short, have mostly been supported on a partial basis by a range of professions and agencies. Their sense of belonging to one or more 'communities', whether that is the local neighbourhood or a network of friends, has rarely been the subject of a comprehensive, strategic approach by professionals. Rather, each agency has sought to maximise the support and expertise they can give children from within their own particular remit and from a specific perspective. A holistic approach has been missing. This is a crucially important point when taking seriously the theme of children and communities.

Interestingly, the above analysis is much less convincing when the theme of children and communities is put in the context of the developing world. In development programmes, awareness of the extent of poverty, and the need to make connections between school, health, literacy and other programmes, has led to a growing recognition that genuine partnerships between agencies' programmes and local communities is imperative. UNICEF argues that effective primary health care depends on there being active communities which press for services and which are involved in deciding how they are delivered.

UNICEF also goes some way towards recognising that community empowerment is a necessary condition of sustainable development. In campaigns aimed at protecting working children, the efforts of children themselves are gaining more notice. Tacon (1991, p. 96), for example, refers to a national conference in Brazil of over 400 street children where: workshops and other activities were largely planned and managed by a co-ordinating group of street children. Jo Boyden makes a strong case for an increase in preventive action and community outreach:

> This implies a far greater role than at present for government and municipal authorities and for community and voluntary

groups. It also implies a far more direct involvement for children themselves in planning, management and implementation. (Boyden, 1991, p. 134)

Within other European countries there are likely to be both policy and practice developments which are relevant to the UK context. In France, for example, local children's councils have become an accepted part of civic life in more than 700 towns. The national association describes a council as 'a place of suggestion, of exchange, of dialogue between adolescents and the authorities'. Representatives are elected and they raise issues with adult local authority elected representatives who thus have a means of listening to children's opinions and acting on them. A small number of children's councils, based on the French model, have been established in Britain. This example illustrates the potential learning to be gained by groups across Europe, and the need for there to be lobbies and networks, linked to the European Commission, which can put the case for children's participation in matters which directly influence their lives in neighbourhoods. Recognising a European perspective on community-based approaches to working with children, combined with the views of experts and of children themselves, could be important in terms of developing the theme of children and communities.

Child and Childhood

We live in a rapidly ageing society. At the beginning of this century, children (aged 0 to 15) accounted for around one-third of the population in most European countries. Today the figure is already below 20 per cent in several countries. The combined effect of lower birth rates and rising life expectancy is changing the relationship between generations.

Community practitioners – playworkers, youth and community workers – frequently come face to face with generational tensions and conflicts. This can take the form of children playing outside the ground floor flats of elderly people, some of whom object to the noise. Or children 'hang around' shopping areas or other public places. What is essential 'togetherness' for one generational group is threatening to another. In many instances, skilled practitioners can work with and harness the agendas of both groups – the energy of children and the wish of adults to help create facilities for children. In recent years, however, such consensual methods have become more difficult to apply because of the breakdown of trust between children and adults.

There is little evidence that the changes resulting from an ageing society, and their impact on the lives of children outside the family and school, are being addressed. The assumptions in the policy formulation processes remain strongly individualistic. They seek to help or treat the child independently from his or her 'community' of friends, networks, neighbours, playspace, alleyways, shopping arcades. The same applies to children as a group. They are regarded as a collection of separate individuals, akin to a random collection of atoms, rather than as a group which has the potential to develop an identity of its own. The heart of the issue is a failure by adults to engage with the issue of power as it relates to children. They have given children more responsibilities, and placed them under increasing commercial and other pressures. What they have not done is to analyse ways in which children could legitimately and helpfully use power.

Social scientists, on the other hand, have shown more interest in exploring the idea of children being part of society. Jens Quortrup, writing about a major research project of the European Centre for Social Welfare Policy and Research, urges us to consider childhood in a societal context: 'How does the *single* child develop *into* a responsible, capable, competent and mature *human being*? How do we manage to integrate children into our modern world?' (Quortrup, 1991). He suggests that the prevailing concerns of preparing children for their adult lives and of protecting them against dangers tend to reduce the attention given to broader issues which may help us to understand the phenomenon of childhood:

> In our project we contend that children *belong* to society – not in the trivial sense of simply being there, nor as a reduced form of raw material to be moulded, nor as the possession of the society or the state. Childhood is part of society in the sense that children do in fact participate in organised activities, and it constitutes a part of the social structure interacting in many ways with other parts. (Quortrup, 1991, p. 14)

The approach of this research is at a theoretical level and has a particular interest in the relationship between generations, and the change in childhood from one historical period to another. Yet it relates powerfully to the theme of children and communities in at least three senses: it places children as the central unit of observation by researchers; it has an overriding interest in studying the extent to which children can speak and act for themselves; and it is informed by a sociological rather than a psychological framework.

The last point in particular emphasises the experiences of children and the concept of childhood outside the framework of the family. It explores children's worlds of school, sense of place, leisure and employment from a 'community' perspective. It begins to identify the conceptual 'territory' on which the contributions to this volume are based.

A close reading of the contributions provides important evidence for a key principle required in order to work effectively with children in a community context. The need for a holistic approach, of seeing and understanding children in their totality, from individual circumstances to environmental conditions has been referred to already, and this is based on the principle of the indivisibility of need: the argument that particular needs cannot be separated from each other because they are experienced interdependently. Accordingly, the approach of professional agencies interested in working with children in the community context cannot be undertaken on a partial basis. 'Need' in the context of working with children has to go beyond the concept of social exclusion. It must be given a sufficiently broad definition to embrace children's sense of fun and enjoyment, their interests, and their concerns about both local and global matters.

Children and Participation

Participation is authentic when we are aware that we count for something and when we feel confident about contributing to discussion. Participation takes on real meaning when what we say is listened to and acted upon. Ultimately participation leads us to have more control over our lives, or at least to have the prospect of more control.

This meaning of participation is of major importance in community development. Community development is openly biased towards finding ways of reaching those people who have either had very minimal experience of participation or who have found it to be an alienating experience. Accordingly participation is a value which informs and permeates practice, and it applies as strongly to work with children as to work with adults. Participation reveals children to be active agents, not consumers.

A reading of the UN Convention on the Rights of the Child (1989) should make for optimism that participation is being taken seriously at the policy level: 'There is, at least in rhetoric, significant growth in the establishment of principles and procedures designed to involve children in decision-making forums' (Smith, 1992). Article 12 deals with the child's right to express his or her opinions; article 13 the right to freedom of expression; article 15 the right of freedom of association; article 31 the right to leisure, recreation and cultural activities. Yet the Convention provides only a legal and policy framework; it does not guarantee that the rights will necessarily be established. As Jim Radford points out in his chapter below, policies and resources of agencies, good practice, pressure and support are needed to begin to enable children to take action themselves. Participation is a general term. It has to be analysed and explored in different, overlapping settings.

We have to make the conceptual link between a quasi-legislative document like the Convention and the establishment of participatory rights in the community context. This has two aspects: the extent to which children can participate together, rather than as separate individuals, in participatory activities; and experience participation in a community, whether that be a shared geographical area or a common interest. Participation is not only a very broad concept, it is also highly 'flexible'. At the extreme, it is possible to envisage participation of children in the issues highlighted in the Convention taking place on a wholly individualised and privatised basis. This would undoubtedly be a very limited form of empowerment.

The key to ensuring that children's participation can take more of a collective form in community settings lies in the community development process. Essentially this means conceiving work with children in terms of a number of stages, in each of which the needs and interests of groups being supported remain paramount. It is a process which, as Heaton and Sayer (1992) point out, offers much more than a method of prevention: 'It offers a framework through which the services can achieve their goal of participation and partnership' (p. 25). Key to it is its capacity to bring children and adults together. Given the degree of adult ignorance of children's concerns, highlighted for example in research by the Centre for Criminology at Edinburgh University

(1992), the relevance of this contribution cannot be stressed too highly.

There are many opportunities for supporting children's participation through application of the community development process. By 'community development process' I mean the stages of development through which community groups and their members move as a result of involvement in local action. It is an educative experience which is at the heart of community development. It is therefore important to make the process a priority. For this to happen the attitudes of adults towards children are critical. Taking the example of Save the Children, alongside its development of family centres it is paying more attention to ways in which children and young people can be directly included in the design, operation and management of its projects as well as in the services provided for children. Examples include the introduction of children's voice time in family centres, interviews with young traveller children about the kind of play provision they would like, community health work with children and young people to give them a say on decisions on health issues, wide consultation with children in Northern Ireland about the content of a Charter for Play, and the involvement of children in the design and development of new provision, e.g. adventure playgrounds. SCF has identified the following issues arising from the search for greater involvement of children in its work:

- Children and young people need to be clear about what is on offer and what is expected of them. They need to know the limits of their influence on decision making and, like adults in the same process, the limits to operating a community development model from within a large, national, policy-led voluntary organisation. They need good, accessible information and personal support if they are to become genuinely involved.
- Different working methods will have to be developed so that children are not simply expected to learn adult methods. Adults must learn new methods to involve children and young people properly. Such methods will need to be different for different groups and purposes, and will need to work with the inevitable turnover of members in such groups.
- Participation can become burdensome to participants and may meet the agency's needs better than those of children and young people. Continual care will have to be taken to bear in mind what it means for those involved.

- Encouraging participation can be costly and time consuming and will have significant financial and practical implications for the agency, which must be budgeted for.
- All meetings and events involving children and young people must be pre-planned in a way which clearly identifies their purpose, the children and young people's role and what will happen to the outcomes. All participants must have safeguards about how their views will count.
- Encouraging the participation of children and young people will affect the work done by this agency. How far is it prepared to go in giving up its control over agenda setting?
- Consideration must be given to involving all groups and not just the 'easy' ones. (Bell, 1993)

Children and Neighbourhoods

If we take neighbourhood to mean the immediate streets where a child lives, we still need to recognise the complexity and over-lapping interests which exist within a neighbourhood:

> A neighbourhood is an area where the majority of people know by sight most of those who live there and probably recognise everyone of their own age group; know all the significant buildings and the central focus of the area – shops, schools, libraries, children's playgrounds, clinics, surgeries, youth clubs, Bingo halls, pubs or whatever. (Seabrook, 1984)

Neighbourhoods are part of children's environment, yet there is mounting evidence that children are being denied access to them. Fear of attack, danger from traffic, concerns about drugs and crime are some of the factors which explain this trend. Some neighbourhoods in inner-city areas evoke the language and culture of fear, violence and despair to a degree that 'comfortable Britain' finds incomprehensible:

> 'It's terrible, your windows get smashed and everything' (eight year old); 'They get cars from outside your doors – they done that three times outside ours. And they take cars down the Tyne and burn them out. And there's gluesniffers' (eight year old). (Wallace, 1992)

Whatever the circumstances of children's neighbourhoods, the interconnections of issues is becoming increasing evident. Craig

Russell, in his analysis of Moss Side and Hulme below argues convincingly that unless strong connections are made between racism, unemployment, drugs and policing, community development strategies for work with children will always fail

The neighbourhood will mean different things for different aged children, but common to all of them will be a need for territory and for belonging. I have referred earlier to the reluctance of community workers to place children at the top of the agenda in their practice, and this is certainly curious given the dominance of neighbourhood work within British community development and the ways in which children's activities have been used as a way in to working on 'adult' issues. The development of family centres, and the more recent emergence of child care facilities run by community enterprises, are helping to rectify this situation. There is also recognition of how action taken by adults – campaigning for a pedestrian crossing, maintaining a community centre, constructing a playground – can be models of behaviour for children:

> The local response to community issues, pressures and needs have an impact on the values, morals and images available to the child. This material is ready to be used later on in their lives when it may be used to create more abstract concepts. (Hasler, 1988)

In making the case for the importance of the neighbourhood, Thomas (1986) and others are aware that neighbourhood action and neighbourhood work are not panaceas for resolving the issue of participation in community life. Indeed, the growth in recent years of identity groups, notably of black groups and of people with disabilities, has given a sharper, more creative meaning to the idea of interest groups – associations and movements which unite people across neighbourhoods, not only within them. Yet as far as children are concerned, the neighbourhood has a reality which is tangible and dramatic, and the scope for acknowledging the rights of children on a neighbourhood basis is immense. Indeed, if an agency or practitioner is aiming to involve children on a collective basis, the neighbourhood is likely to yield more positive results than a more generalised concern with children's participation. The latter will tend to foster a more individual emphasis – the empowerment of the child as opposed to the development of children – because it lacks the solid, shared and accessible basis offered by the neighbourhood.

Policy and Practice

The development of community-based work with children, unsur-
prisingly has been based on practice. It is practitioners who have
both the experience and the opportunities to see the relevance
and potential of different working methods. They will also tend
to be strongly committed to finding ways of ensuring that the
value basis of their practice finds expression in a number of
forms. This will often include participation and the neighbourhood as resources.

Practitioners observe the strengths and weaknesses of neighbourhoods and can assess the advantages and disadvantages of
community-based forms of practice. Those people concerned
with influencing public policies, on the other hand, do not
experience the immediacy of the neighbourhood. Research, too,
is cast in a questioning, supportive but distanced role compared
with the daily tasks and challenges in which practitioners are
immersed.

However, stating that a policy lag is to be expected is one
thing; suggesting that it need not engage with the issue of children
and communities is quite another. Arguably, it will only be when
practice becomes linked with policy, and hence with the prospect
of resources, that new forms of practice can move beyond being
dependent upon the enthusiasm and energies of a minority of
practitioners. Practice needs legitimation, support and encouragement at policy level.

While legislation can provide the framework for policy formulation, it is the combination of central government guidelines
to local authorities and the internal management systems of
agencies themselves which need to be activated. For the first of
these, lobbying organisations have a clear role to play in terms
of seeking to influence senior civil servants and ministers. With
regard to the second, it is a question of establishing dialogue
between practitioners and managers, with the middle manager
being in a pivotal position to influence both groups.

If we return to the example of the child care organisations, we
can see the interrelationship between practice and policy illustrated. The Children's Society's director, in describing the
development of practice, notes that, 'as the new practice developed,
we realised that it was beginning to establish *principles* which
affected the way in which the Society was organised and managed'
(Sparks, 1988). And the society's social policy officer points out

that responding to the wishes and needs expressed directly by children themselves may change the focus of the organisation's work. He compares a possible contrasting list of issues when they are considered from the child's rather than the adult's viewpoint:

Children's issues	*Adult issues*
1. Access to play	1. Coping with kids
2. Feeling left out (poverty)	2. Managing the home
3. School	3. Coping with stress
4. Safety	4. Day care
5. Bullying	5. Employment

(Smith, 1992)

The development of community-based services in Barnardo's indicates a movement over time from practice to policy similar to that of the Children's Society, Save the Children and NCH Action for Children. Dixon, in outlining the development in Barnardo's, notes that there is no uniformity of project types:

> We have single workers on single estates and we have large project teams spanning several estates within a local authority area; we have family centres that employ a community development approach and we have churches and community projects that will use the methods alongside a range of other approaches. (Dixon, 1992)

Barnardo's corporate plan approved by its council in 1991 is informed both by its community development experiences – notably the Osmondthorpe project in Leeds (Wolinski, 1986) – and its internal policy development work.

Whether or not a similar dynamic between policy and community practice can be established within both statutory agencies and other child care organisations is less certain. The development of community social work at the beginning of the 1980s, whereby social work teams adopted a neighbourhood approach, ran into the sands. Advocates of this approach are currently reassessing the situation in the light of the expansion of specialisms and recent legislation.

The history of community development in Britain and the US is dominated by a 'project' ethos: the setting up of a small number of short-life projects from which it is hoped lessons will be drawn for policy formulation. More often than not this has been a forlorn hope. For a number of reasons it appears to be very difficult to make projects successful using that criterion. They tend to have been more successful in the local situation and, in some cases, with regard to influencing local authorities. National community development agencies realised that a complementary strategy was required – influencing public policy – by using a range of dissemination tools: policy reports, seminars, conferences, research, information, etc.

A similar analysis can be applied to the theme of children and communities. Attention has to be given to policy influence in addition to promoting and supporting practice. Otherwise there is a danger of the issue remaining in a cul de sac. The lobbying undertaken for a children's rights commissioner, the national strategy on the UN Convention undertaken by the Children's Rights Development Unit, and the campaign to provide comprehensive protection for children in all settings (Gulbenkian Foundation, 1993) all provide good models of how national policy work on children's issues can be effective. Such work can take place in the European and international contexts too. It is essential that the European Community's concern with social exclusion includes issues being experienced by children – poverty, violence, inadequate play facilities, etc.

Conclusion

So far I have refrained from specifying an age range of children with which the book is concerned. This reluctance reflects a preference for avoiding rigid categorisations. Community development is interested in making connections between individuals and groups in society, in helping them identify what they have in common, not reinforcing those things that keep people separate.

It is a similar working principle to that of the indivisibility of need discussed earlier: cross-cutting issues, a broad definition of need, an intergenerational perspective. These approaches may be frustrating to specialist organisations, and they may promise more than they can deliver, but within them there lies the kernel of the book's theme.

The challenge is to create a more balanced relationship between agencies which have responsibilities for the education and welfare of children and the communities where children live. Wood puts the point in more ambitious terms:

> Childhood in the 21st century will, if trends remain as they
> are, depend on clear understandings between the State and
> its services and the community, and on the growing reali-
> sation that they must work in a mutually beneficial
> partnership. (Wood, 1991)

Achieving such a partnership will require agencies and policy
makers to consider children's future with a mixture of vision and
modesty: they need to see the scope for releasing the energy and
goodwill which exists among children and adults in communities, and they need to listen more attentively to the voices of
children themselves – how they feel they can participate, what
the neighbourhood means to them, how the time and skills of
professional practitioners can be better supported by their agencies.

On the other hand, the subject matter of this book is important
because there is such a long way to go. We are only beginning to
explore how children can play a more active part in society and
we are doing this in a context of severe inequality and injustice
for children. To an extent, therefore, readers have to go beyond
the three ideas I have outlined. A conceptual and imaginative leap
is needed between present-day realities and future possibilities.
The contributions which follow have been chosen on that basis.
They are there to push forward the exploration, to provide a
stimulus for further discussion and study.

A wish for the book to be characterised by a breadth of issues
and disciplines led me to structure it in four parts and to include
both policy and practice issues in each part. The concluding
chapter by Peter Newell is designed to be absorbed whether or not
all the preceding chapters have been read, and linking passages
have been provided to help identify the context of each part. In
this way it is hoped that the contents will be accessible to a wide
range of readers, who will be able to make their own connections
with the overall theme.

References

Adams, R. (1991) *Protest by Pupils: Empowerment, Schooling and the
   State*, London: The Falmer Press.
Aldridge, J. and Becker, S. (1993) *Children Who Care – Inside the
   World of Young Carers*, Loughborough: Loughborough University

in association with Nottinghamshire Association of Voluntary Organisations.

Baldock, P. (1983) 'Community Development and Community Care' in *Community Development Journal*, vol. 1, no. 3.

Bell, B. (1993) 'Children in Communities', mimeo, London: Save the Children.

Boyden, J. (1991) *Children of the Cities*, London: Zed Books.

Centre for Criminology, Edinburgh University (1992) *Cautionary Tales*, University of Edinburgh.

Clinton, L. and Glen, A. (1993) 'Community Arts' in Butcher, H. et al. (eds) *Community and Public Policy*, London: Pluto Press.

Comedia (1991) *Out of Hours: A Study of Social and Cultural Life in 12 Town Centres in the UK*, London: Comedia.

Dixon, N. (1992) 'The Evolution of Barnardo Policies in Relation to Children and Communities', mimeo, Barkingside: Barnardo's.

Gibbons, J. (1990) *Family Support and Prevention: Studies in Local Areas*, London: NISW/HMSO.

Guichard, S. and Ader, J. (1991) 'La Ville a jouer – Donner une place a l'enfant dans l'espace public' in *Arch. & Comport/Arch. Behav.*, vol. 7, no. 2, pp. 123–36.

Gulbenkian Foundation (1993) *One Scandal Too Many*, London: Calouste Gulbenkian Foundation.

Harlesden Community Project (1979) *Community Work and Caring for Children*, Ilkley: Owen Wells.

Hasler, J. (1988) 'Community Development – Is it Child Care?' in *Working with Communities*, ed. P. Henderson, London: The Children's Society.

Heaton, K. and Sayer, J. (1992) *Community Development and Child Welfare*, London: CDF Publications/in association with The Children's Society.

Mayo, M. (1975) 'The History and Early Development of CDP' in *Action-Research in Community Development*, ed. R. Lees and G. Smith, London: Routledge & Kegan Paul.

Quortrup, J. (1991) *Childhood as a Social Phenomenon – An Introduction to a Series of National Reports*, Vienna: European Centre for Social Welfare Policy and Research.

Seabrook, J. (1984) *The Idea of Neighbourhood*, London: Pluto Press.

Shaw, R. (1989) *Prisoners' Children*, London: Routledge.

Smith, B. (1993) 'The Effect of Long-Term Unemployment on People's Lives' in *Beyond Unemployment*, Respond! (98 Dovecot Street, Stockton-on-Tees, Cleveland TS18 1HA).

Smith, R. (1992) 'Recent Developments: The Rights of Children', mimeo, London: The Children's Society.

Sparks, I. (1988) 'Community Development and the Organisation' in *Children and Communities*, ed. P. Henderson, London: The Children's Society.

Tacon, P. (1991) 'A Global Overview of Social Mobilisation on Behalf of Street Children' in *Protecting Working Children*, ed. W.E. Myers, London: Zed Books.

Thomas, D.N. (1983) *The Making of Community Work*, London: George Allen & Unwin.

Thomas, D.N. (1986) *White Bolts Black Locks*, London: George Allen & Unwin.

UN Convention on the Rights of the Child (1989).

Wallace, B. (1992) 'Living on the Edge' in *Social Work Today*, 16 January.

Warner, M. (1989) *Into the Dangerous World*, London: Chatto & Windus.

Warner, M. (1994) 'Little Angels, Little Devils', third of Reith Lectures, *Managing Monsters*, London: BBC.

Wolinski, A. (1986) *Osmundthorpe: The Area That Time Forgot*, London: Barnardos.

Wood, F. (1991) 'Community Mobilisation' in *Newsletter*, Bernard van Leer Foundation, no. 63, July.

Part 1 Care and Protection

The neglect of children by wealthy countries is becoming increasingly stark. Sylvia Hewlett (1993), writing on this theme for UNICEF, suggests that over the last 15 years two approaches to child welfare have emerged:

> a neglect-filled 'Anglo-American' model, where market-driven public policies have slashed family benefits and gone a long way towards privatising child-rearing; and a much more supportive 'European' model, where governments have strengthened rather than weakened safety nets for families with children.

The UK and the US have higher child poverty rates than France, Germany, the Netherlands, Sweden, Australia and Canada.

Pressures on children and families in the UK increased significantly during the 1980s. More children have experienced poverty and homelessness and, notably in some inner-city areas and outer estates, they have had to survive in a more fearful and threatened society. Children are the most obvious victims of a wider social crisis induced not because the country is poor but because it has become less equal. Children and families have been pushed down the priorities list, and comfortable Britain has allowed this to happen.

This is the context in which a critique of social welfare policies on children has to be located. The facts that the proportion of children on child protection registers set up by local authorities almost quadrupled during the 1980s, and that the numbers of young children taken into care also increased, are as much a reflection of society's abdication of responsibilities as of government and local authority policies towards children.

One purpose of raising questions about the care and protection of children in the community – the theme of this part of the book – is to remind us of the importance of the wider debate about the rights of 13 million children, keeping on the political agenda the theme of opportunities for children and the ways in which adults can help them to grow and develop. If this perspective is absent then the picture for the social welfare approach to the care and protection of children is bleak indeed. The siege mentality of most social services and social work departments, springing in particular from the Cleveland Child Abuse enquiry, appears to be today's reality. The time and energy of social workers and their managers is consumed with following procedures and checking and double-checking possible abuse cases.

Apart from being demoralising, to remain trapped in this framework will, in the end, be self-defeating. Somehow local authorities have to find ways of getting off the treadmill of protection and policing and rediscover strategies aimed at prevention. This is where the community moves back to centre stage for social workers and others. It is untenable for agencies to remain distanced from the lives and neighbourhoods of children and their families, especially when government-funded research on family support (Gibbons, 1992) points to the positive outcomes arising from family centres and other community resources.

This is the 'territory' which the following three chapters occupy, the first two through discussions of practice, and the third at a theoretical level. All three are seeking to pull back into the policy area the benefits and scope of having community development and prevention as powerful components of child care and protection. In this sense they represent a minority position in the child care and protection field, swimming against the prevailing tide, at least within the crisis-dominated statutory services. There are examples of social services/social work teams adopting a preventive approach to child care, and these have been upheld by a network of social workers and trainers supporting community social work. The examples, however, are few and it is no accident that the three chapters in this volume have a strong voluntary sector ethos to them. This reflects the continuing commitment of national voluntary organisations to supporting children in the community context.

The story of the Family Service Unit's Neighbourhood Centre in Leeds demonstrates how, even within the tightly drawn guidelines of government circulars and the pressures on social services departments which result in the provision only of a fire brigade service, it is possible to be innovative and creative. The project is an example of exploiting the 'nooks and crannies' within a large local authority, including the support of individual elected members and staff. It also depicts the complex web within which such a small local project has to operate: staff, committee members and users of the project linked to a national voluntary organisation, and negotiating financial support with the local authority. At the same time it seeks to develop and maintain links with local groups and networks.

A key question in some readers' minds will concern the involvement of children in the planning of activities at the neighbourhood centre. Are the activities too adult determined? Are we still too hesitant about allowing children responsibility? The same question can be asked of the second contribution, Kanchan Jadeja's chapter on black children in care: was there not scope, in the example given of the Asian women's group, for children to organise on their own behalf?

The dominance of casework in 'Black Children in Care' makes it hard for the chapter's content to be ignored by mainstream service providers. It crosses the uncertain border country between the cultures and traditions of black communities and the assumptions and procedures of social services/social work departments. The implications, therefore, of the chapter's material present a challenge to agencies genuinely committed to anti-racist policies and practices.

Teresa Smith's contribution is pitched at a theoretical and policy level. In addition to reviewing the research evidence on children and poverty she discusses the child as 'active learner/active participant', placing this in a broader framework of empowerment and participation. Her argument for interpreting the Children Act 1989 in preventive, community-based terms gives this part of the book an optimistic note. She reasserts the case for applying community work principles to work with children, not primarily because this will strengthen social work and community work but because it will benefit children.

The three chapters give us a glimpse of alternative scenarios to a control-dominated child care and protection system. They also make the vitally important links between child care, poverty and racism. Thus they represent an aspect of the children and community theme with which policy makers urgently need to engage.

References

Hewlett, S.A. (1993) *Child Neglect in Rich Nations*, New York: UNICEF.

Gibbons, J. ed. (1992) *The Children Act 1989 and Family Support: Principles into Practice*, London: HMSO.

1 A Neighbourhood Centre – Protection and Prevention

Roger Barford, Sarah O'Grady and Ruth Hall

How can adults respond to children's own definition of their needs, as opposed to creating adult interpretations of those needs? This question is especially pertinent for social workers because they have specific statutory duties and responsibilities for the care and protection of children, and we have been very aware of this when relating our own experiences. At the same time we believe that the needs of children cannot be understood in isolation from their peers, families and neighbourhoods. Whether or not this means that the project we discuss here involved working on an agenda agreed to the exclusion, wholly or partially, of children-defined issues, we leave the reader to consider.

The chapter will examine the development and work of a neighbourhood project in the inner city of Leeds run by a national voluntary organisation. The focus of the project's work has always been child protection, but the definition of protection and methods of work have focused on protection through prevention, and a commitment to work to the strengths of both individual families and local community networks (see Johnson, 1993).

West Leeds Family Service Unit (FSU) is part of a national organisation which consists of 20 separate units spread throughout the UK. Each unit has a local management committee to whom the staff are accountable for their practice, which is carried out in line with the policies of the national organisation. The units work autonomously but with similar goals centred on working with families living in disadvantaged communities. A variety of approaches are used by the different units, ranging from intensive therapeutic individual work to community social work.

The Project

The area of Leeds where the project is sited is designated an inner-city improvement area. It consists of small terraced housing, some back-to-back and often poorly maintained, built at the beginning of this century. The housing stock is partly council, partly private landlord owned, the latter often in multi-occupation. The immediate neighbourhood of the project has a significant Asian population characterised by young families. There is also an identifiable but mobile student population in the locality. The area is generally under-resourced and child care provision (both statutory and private) is poor. For children and adults in many local families racial harassment is a daily occurrence.

The project was funded by the local authority social services and health departments through joint finance, in response to the increase in numbers of children on the child protection register. A neighbourhood model was identified in the original brief, but there was nothing explicit about the fact that this would require different methods of work and models of practice. Inevitably this led to tensions between the type of project that was eventually established, and the more accepted definitions of child protection work which focus on 'abuse'.

The start of the project coincided with implementation of the 1989 Children Act, which again represented a shift in emphasis and definition. Local authorities were required to define and provide services for children in need, meaning all children rather than only those identified as being at risk.

There was a new responsibility to involve families by working in partnership with them – implicit recognition that families have knowledge and skills in respect of the care of their children. This recognition in statute provided a further rationale for the model the project developed to build on the strengths and networks of families and neighbourhoods.

The direction in which the project developed was further assisted by FSU's involvement nationally in clients' rights, together with a well-established record on equality of opportunity and anti-oppressive practice. This did much to underpin working practices as they developed. The anti-racist work, for example, complemented the shift from casework to a more holistic approach where the focus of intervention is not the family alone but also the extended family and the local community. Utilising and building on the strengths of people and their community is integral to this approach.

The project's local management committee, as part of FSU's management structure, was formed when the project was being developed. The members had a commitment to supporting and understanding a model of work that took a different approach to established practice both locally and in FSU itself. There were tensions and differences in understanding about the extent to which the project should become community oriented, but overall the project team was supported in its development and style of work.

The result was a project located in an ordinary terraced house (extended) in a well-defined neighbourhood seen to possess many of the recognised indices of deprivation, and where young families were potentially at risk as a consequence of the environmental and structural stresses placed on them. The project team developed open access, open door services (e.g. drop-in, toy library, advice work), together with a structured group work programme for children (e.g. after-school provision), adults (women and violence, Asian women's development) and children and adults together (e.g. parent and carers' group). After almost two years of running these services from the project base staff developed a referral system in conjunction with the local social services team to undertake time-limited work with particular referred families who would then hopefully be able to begin to use the other services provided by the project.

As the project and this work developed, the team itself was con-solidating the value base from which its aims, objectives and performance indicators were derived. This was undertaken as a collective and collaborative exercise from the outset, which gave the team cohesion and a sense of direction. It was facilitated by the fact that the team was initially small (six members) and stable: it existed with virtually no changes for its first two years. Alongside this planning, team building, staff development and training were made available to the team as a whole, on areas directly relevant to their service delivery. The project team, in turn, developed resources for local people and the community in the form of newsletters, community lunches, shared training resources, and access to and use of project resources, as well as the more structured group work programme.

The project believes that this style of work provides a local community with increased resources with which adults can

protect themselves and their children. Services are non-stigma-
tising; they are not identified by problem definition, and the roles
and boundaries between consumer and service provider become
much more blurred and interchangeable. For example, a service
user may also be a volunteer and a member of the management
committee over a period of time. This characteristic of the project
also means that boundaries between professional and community
networks become less clearly defined and can produce tensions
and conflict for workers, particularly in their relationship with
statutory agencies. The following examples of the project's work
demonstrate its philosophy and practice.

Summer Playschemes

We have run playschemes with the help of the local community
since we arrived in this area in 1989. They are for children aged
5 to 12 years and take place each summer.

The initial request came from parents and children who were
already using our toy library and open door services only weeks
after the project opened. The request for summer activities was
backed up by local schools and the social services department who
were very concerned at the lack of space and facilities for children's
play and recreation in the area.

At the outset of planning we decided to use local people as
helpers, including teenagers who were interested in working with
children and who often came bringing younger brothers and
sisters. Over the years this has developed well and almost all
playscheme helpers are now local parents. One of our main aims
in running the playschemes has been to ensure that they involve
a mix of children and workers which reflects the ethnic make-up
of the area. We have achieved this every year and it ensures that
the atmosphere on the scheme is friendly to children from all
cultures.

We help the children to draw up rules at the start of each
scheme which address issues of racism and sexism in a simple way,
e.g. no name-calling. All the activities we provide help to show
positive images of black people and girls/women. We use books
and tapes with Urdu translations and Afro-Caribbean fairy stories.
We provide Asian games, black dolls and ethnic dressing-up
clothes. The children are involved in multi-cultural cookery and
enjoy Mendhi (hand-painting) and face-painting in preparation

for the party. We employ Kuffdem, a black theatre group which addresses topical issues through drama.

We have learned to take our lead from the children as to which activities to provide. They are quick to tell us what they have most enjoyed and leave some activities almost untouched. We encourage them to make suggestions and hope to allow for a flexibility of response within what is, of necessity, a structured framework.

We have used video with some success in our evaluation process and produced a video of the scheme for fundraising purposes. It was shown to the parents and children who had participated, and we always aim to build on the response we get from parents and children in our planning for future schemes.

There can be no doubt that our schemes go some way to protecting local children. We hold a number of places for children identified by social services as being at risk. It is also clear that black children enjoy the safety of the scheme where they are not exposed to the racist abuse which many of them suffer on the local streets. By involving parents as workers we raise abilities which in turn must be of benefit to their children. We have also found that families whose initial contact with us has been through the playscheme have moved on to become involved in other activities, such as the toy library and fundraising.

Single Parent Group

The single parent group started in response to the needs of local parents and pressures from local agencies who were working with families.

The early stages of planning the group involved parents who were interested in being members, and workers from FSU and a nearby community centre. This preliminary planning produced a model for the group whereby it would be an open group aimed at building and maintaining supportive relationships between group members. To promote these the group would meet regularly, would have a variety of approaches, and the workers would use their skills and knowledge to gain resources for the group, to help achieve members' ideas for the group and to facilitate the running of the sessions.

From the point of view of FSU, the group was also an important part of our strategy of inter-agency work, developing links with other local projects that had complementary aims, sharing

resources and skills and thereby providing a fuller, more comprehensive set of services for the community. Our space was very
cramped, and the two free rooms at the community centre offered
a space for the group and the crèche which FSU could not have
provided alone. The staff, one Asian female crèche worker, one
Asian female first from community education and then from
FSU, and one white male project worker, contributed a range of
backgrounds, interests and skills, broadening and deepening the
possibilities of the group.

We also gained and used information about resources in and
outside Leeds to use during group sessions and to increase their
general availability to group members as knowledge and confidence
grew.

Group sessions offered a warm, welcoming, reliable meeting
place, a place for a chat and a place for personal issues to be aired.
Group members would share experiences and offer mutual support
in sorting out difficulties, as well as using the knowledge of the
workers. We had a crèche throughout to guarantee an uninter-
rupted break for parents, though we also had sessions of fun
activities for parents and children, both in term time and holidays.
Participants came from a range of ethnic backgrounds and we made
sure discussions were translated so that all could understand
what was going on. We learnt and shared skills in playing games,
cookery, jewellery and pottery. We shared DIY, gardening and child
care tasks. These sessions necessitated gaining information about
resources in and outside Leeds, which was useful both for the group
as a whole and broadened the facilities available to group members
as their self-esteem and confidence grew. Thus negotiations with
local schools and churches for use of their premises during
holidays, arranging to use Community Transport minibuses,
planning teaching sessions on health, crafts and beauty all opened
new possibilities and gave group members an experience of
achieving a response to their needs. An apparently impervious
local authority would open up buildings and would give funds
when approached by parents with sufficient conviction and
support from the group.

The whole group planned and raised funds for a week's holiday
for four of the families. The planning and the holiday itself were
a shared experience of the joys and strains of meeting diverse adult
and child needs, of mutual co-operation and enjoyment, and of
the boundaries to that.

The group's initial recruits were parents and its initial focus was on how to meet their needs. Throughout the group we recognised the importance of responding to what the children involved needed, as perceived by the adults. Thus the crèche offered a friendly, stimulating place to play, but the group was flexible enough for children to be allowed into the 'adults'' room, or for parents to stay with their children if that's what they needed. Meetings in the centre were interspersed with outings to places the children enjoyed and which may have been inaccessible to parents on their own and without transport. School holidays offered a wider age range of children, and discussions with them and with their parents led to activities enjoyable for this more diverse group: train trips to a water park, craft workshops, a museum trip and ball games in the local park, and the holiday. Here, as elsewhere, there were conflicts and compromises about the different needs of individuals within the group, both adults and children: a mother who needed a break, some adult company and adult fun had children who needed adult help to explore the sea and sand; teenage children needed excitement, amusement and noisy late nights; younger ones needed boat trips and castles; parents needed an infinite supply of money; and workers needed to be available to all to negotiate and respond.

So the children involved in the group had their needs recognised and responded to in three distinct ways. The under-fives who came to the crèche during term time were talked to by the workers and by their parents about what they wanted to do. We also reacted to their signs of enjoyment or distress, indications of how successfully we were meeting their needs. In planning holiday-time meetings parents were asked to involve their older children, too, in deciding what activities would be enjoyable, and in order to bring their wishes back to the group, as the workers usually had no direct contact with these children. Inevitably these consultations, trying to meet the differing needs of the different adults and of children across a spread of ages and interests needed some careful resolution to avoid a position that 'adults know best', and to boost the self-esteem of the adults in terms of abilities and worth as parents.

Recruitment of group members took place through leaflets and posters, and through contacts with local workers such as health visitors and teachers. Mostly, however, new members came through personal contacts with existing participants or with the group workers, though they often needed repeated invitation or encouragement to have the confidence to step into an unknown group. Membership also fluctuated with the personal circumstances of members. A drop in numbers after a few months was the result of participants finding jobs and starting new relationships – a blow for the group but positive moves for those involved.

Eventually, 20 months after its initiation, group members decided that they had the experience, the confidence and the back up to become a self-run, self-help group, and embarked on running the group themselves.

It was vital throughout the scheme to involve the children in the families on both sides of the link. The children of single parent families could be direct beneficiaries, with the parent volunteer undertaking activities that were particularly important to him/her. In setting up and supporting the link we made a point of checking with these children on the interests, issues or possibilities that needed to be considered from their point of view. Depending on the age of the children and how well we knew them, this was achieved by the worker asking the children what they wanted out of the scheme, or by asking the parents to do this and feed back the information to us.

It was important to be aware of the impact of the scheme on the volunteer's children, too. Their time, interests and family patterns were changed by their parents' involvement in the scheme, and we ensured during the training that we and the parents had checked the feelings and wishes of the children in relation to their parents possible participation in the scheme.

Community Language Group

This group was initially set up directly in response to an articulated need from the local Asian community. Parents unable to read or write Urdu themselves were concerned that a cultural heritage was being lost, and asked us to set up a language group which now runs twice a week and reaches, on average, 25 children. As this group has developed it has become clear that it is reaching a need beyond simple language teaching. It provides a 'safe' environment in which Asian children receive individual attention in both educational and social terms. Because of the racial abuse, many of the black children are limited to the confines of their often small and overcrowded homes when they are not at school. The community language group has provided these children with a venue for safe and supportive social contact which would otherwise have been unavailable to them.

Children are actively involved in planning and preparing some sessions, in particular the celebration of various festivals, the Eid Mela for example, and parents have become involved in helping to run trips and in fundraising for the group.

Local volunteers who initially staffed the group alongside FSU staff have now become paid sessional workers and take responsibility for the day-to-day running of the sessions. In this way the group has clearly moved from being a 'provided resource' to a 'participant led' and community supported group.

As the group has developed, the number of children requiring individual input, both educationally and socially, has risen. It is clear that this group is working with a number of children who have behavioural problems, and this is an issue of increasing concern for the workers. The approach has shifted from being predominantly educational to offering individual support, concentrating on self-esteem and confidence as much as education.

In terms of child protection this group is clearly meeting a broad need for protection, within the local community, from abuse and harassment. A secondary effect is to alleviate the stress on the families involved by providing 'time out' for the children, which in turn must improve the general health of the families involved.

Commentary

West Leeds FSU was set up as a response to concerns about child protection, at a time when the imminent introduction of the 1989 Children Act encouraged a critical look at what child protection might mean.

The unit's response was to recognise that child protection can and should operate at a variety of levels: it is more than reacting to specific acts by parents or carers, it is about enabling children to live lives where they are not only freed from fear of acts of abuse but have opportunities to develop their potential.

Without denying the harm done to children assaulted by their carers, we recognised and attempted to counter the harm inflicted on children from other sources too:

- racist attacks which resulted in physical harm, fear, and an inability to play outside the house

- lack of play facilities which increased tensions inside crowded houses and deprived children of social and recreational opportunities
- the isolation of families, where parents stuck at home had skills and confidence eroded and lacked support, encouragement and the opportunity to contemplate changes in their lives
- poverty caused by the lack of employment, the lack of skills, confidence and child care to seek employment, and inadequate rates and inaccurate calculations of benefits
- the undermining, ignoring and undervaluing of the diverse cultural heritage the locality could enjoy.

Obviously many of the areas which concerned us most were in relation to the stresses placed on families by the structural poverty in the neighbourhood. Pressures from outside the area are in the main the causes of problems within it.

The issues we list interact with each other, and have causes and effects at interpersonal, institutional and societal levels. We would not claim to have tackled all of these pressures; we would suggest that our work has looked for positive, strengthening ways of tackling some of them, in conjunction with the participants in the project and local neighbourhood networks. This was commensurate with our stated aims and objectives. Moreover it complied with the Children Act guidance: 'The Act gives a positive emphasis to identifying and providing for the child's needs rather than focusing on parental shortcomings in a negative manner' (HMSO, 1991, p. 8).

The project has seen as one of its main goals the empowerment of people in the local community. To this end it is important to take the focus away from failure, and it is vital to build on the strengths of families, both children and adults, in relation to their interaction and their feelings of self-esteem and worth. In terms of the Children Act, our way of working provides supportive evidence for Teresa Smith's argument in Chapter 3 below for a preventative interpretation of the Act. Thus, the playscheme offered play, social and recreational skills to the children involved and to local adults who were volunteers and sessional workers. It provided a space where racism was not acceptable, and where black and white children learned to enjoy that. It provided an experience of empowerment for adults and children, for it ran in response to their requests and adapted to feedback sought from them. The scheme offered parents a break from some of the pressures of child care, and generated and supported links between families. The range of people and activities offered an exploration and celebration of the skills and talents of the locality.

The single parent group provided similar benefits to the children of the parents involved. It also offered adults an opportunity to build supportive relationships with other adults within and outside the group, to increase their self-esteem and self-confidence, to acknowledge and meet some of their needs in having fun and learning skills, and to open up possibilities – either for change or for increased support in carrying on their present patterns.

The community language classes were a response to requests from the local Asian community that local children should not lose a vital part of their heritage. It was another aspect of work to empower adults and children, to hear and acknowledge requests and to use our skills to help mobilise resources to meet those requests.

A project such as this where most of the revenue, apart from what the project raises itself, is from Joint Finance and ultimately from the local authority social services department, will of necessity be constantly balancing competing demands and priorities. On the one hand there is the consumer/neighbourhood definition of appropriate resources and services; on the other, the social services area team is working to meet statutory child care responsibilities with scarce resources. To argue that tertiary and secondary prevention will decrease the number of children at risk of abuse in the longer term is difficult if the demands for primary prevention today cannot be met.

A media climate seeking public accountability does nothing to diminish the demand for a balancing act, even where the community networks local to the project are in support of its work. To argue the additional benefits and consequences arising for local children from a community language class, as described, is difficult when the opposing argument could be that teaching Urdu is not an appropriate task for project workers and could be undertaken by the education department.

Our view is that we must undertake this kind of work if we are to be seen by local people as being genuinely responsive to what they are telling us about the children. Throughout its work the project has used inter-agency co-operation to build its resources of skills, people and finance, and has used that supportive base to press for wider improvements in agency response. In other words we developed inter-agency work at two levels: building trust and joint initiatives with staff from a range of agencies in the area; and seeking to influence the thinking and policies of senior officers and elected members.

The project has developed links on a neighbourhood level with the education department (both local schools and tertiary education), local health visitors, church groups and social services. Many of our groups have been co-run with other agencies and this has resulted in a sharing of both skills and finance and has offered a more cohesive service to the local community. It has also raised the profile of the project with the senior management structure of other agencies and in some cases helped to empower their workers, enabling them to improve professional practice. It was especially important to maintain a positive dialogue with social services: the project was perceived as being out of the ordinary and, because of its commitment to supporting children on a neighbourhood basis, was seen as working in different ways to local social service teams. We constantly provided evidence of the relevance and effectiveness of our work, and restated the case for supporting groups and networks. In contrast, of necessity, local social services staff worked with individual children and families and could not easily resource work which involved responding to collective needs as expressed at a neighbourhood level, for example, playschemes and after-school activities. Thus it was important to involve local authority social workers in our work as a means of maintaining the dialogue and supporting children in the neighbourhood. Examples of this were their commitment to the staff working on summer playschemes and to co-running time-limited groups with the project.

At times work with participants, adults and children to develop their conception of a useful service may have conflicted and struggled for resources with other local groups, and with local agencies and funders with different priorities or responsibilities. Reorganisation of local schools and the concomitant building work threatened the viability of forthcoming playschemes. While accepting the need and benefits of working co-operatively with other local agencies it is also vital to mention our perspective, to argue our broad view on prevention while our funders in social services are practising a far narrower view. Within the project, running the single parent group through the summer left fewer workers for the summer playscheme; the balance is a matter of competing demands when the project seeks to mediate issues of need, power, skills and resources, while struggling to increase them.

The fact that the project is part of a wider network within a national organisation is important in terms of the project's ability to keep to the agreed remit. Networks develop between units, focusing on shared values and objectives even when their particular styles of work may differ. There is also scope for sharing resources in the form of training, fundraising and skills development. Above all, policies and procedures are developed nationally and then underpin and support locally based work. Local responses from units, particularly in the field of social policy, are likely to have greater impact because they have the professionalism and credibility of being part of a national organisation. This dynamic link between national policy work and local practice has been demonstrated by FSU to be extremely effective for both FSU as a whole and for local units, as in the case of the West Leeds project.

To use and build on people's strengths, to hear and press for validation of their demands, to recognise and respond to the pressures on families, and the particular pressures on those who are single, who are black, who are children, to promote the meeting of children's needs – these aims can seem grandiose. The evidence is more modest: a group of children who now dare to say they will not put up with racial victimisation and assaults; women who recognise their strengths to make positive changes in their lives for jobs, education and new relationships; adults who know they have skills in working creatively with children; families who expect high quality activities for children in the summer, and expect to be constructively critical of them – a very similar approach to that discussed by Joe Hasler in Chapter 10 below. While we have not halted the decline in unemployment, achieved readily available child care or reached affordable benefit levels, some people have more positive control over their lives, and some children are closer to having their needs met. Our aims are perhaps 'to evaluate and to examine the objectives of empowerment and to pay attention to the means of achieving small victories, rather than making harsh judgements about the failure to change the course of history' (Rees, 1991, p. 98).

References

HMSO (1991) *The Children Act 1989 Guidance and Regulations*, vol. 2, London: HMSO.

Johnson, L. (1993) *Families in Partnership: An Independent Evaluation of the West Leeds FSU Neighbourhood Project*, University of Leeds in association with West Leeds FSU Neighbourhood Project.

Rees, S. (1991) *Achieving Power*, London: Allen and Unwin.

2 Black Children in Care

Kanchan Jadeja

Introduction

The black community has responded to racist child care practices of social services departments by developing an approach founded on the need for community-based initiatives. This will be illustrated here through an examination of attempts by black people to develop alternatives to institutional child care services through the adoption of community development methods. In arguing this perspective the following points will be addressed: what is it that goes wrong with the child care provided to black people by social services departments, and how have black people worked together to provide alternatives?

In discussing these questions I shall draw on my own experiences and on those of other black people. There is limited written material available, and Roy (1988) has argued that black people within the child care system have a view of the oppressed which provides a useful and valuable analytical tool. I will rely, too, on the impressions of those involved in social services as workers and consumers: 'Such impressions, although not an adequate substitute for more rigorous enquiry, can nevertheless provide a valuable supplement to that research which is available' (Roy, 1988, p. 209). Inevitably, the chapter presents an adult perspective, but the work of Black and in Care Leicester is an example of adults taking children's perspectives into account.

Community development has played an essential part in the development of black resources through the black voluntary sector (Dutt, 1991; Atkin, 1991). This is as apparent in child care as it is in other social services, for example those concerning black elderly people. Black community development is based on three integrated methods: networking; challenging institutional and other forms of racism; and developing alternative and appropriate resources. All of these methods of working are based on the principle of collective responsibility.

Community development methods are enriched by the tradition of community support that exists in many of the countries of origin of black people, countries where the state's input into social welfare is less apparent then in Britain. When people arrived in this country they brought this tradition with them. People drew on their own economies and resources because the state had not responded to their needs. Sivanandan (1990) has talked about the importance of black people's economy in the support of strikes by black people in Britain. Similarly, local community networks have developed from places of worship, through the setting up of voluntary projects, to applications for grant aid, etc. (Dutt, 1991). The child care services have been incorporated into community centres in the form of playgroups and youth clubs. Black women, especially in the African Caribbean community, have worked at setting up resources for black children in community settings (Small, 1983; Ahmed, 1990).

What Goes Wrong?

In order to look at child care in social services departments we need to analyse racism, and Britain as a racist society. Social services departments and the larger voluntary agencies have failed black children.

> Social workers inspect our families, keep them under sur-
> veillance and in the last resort have the power to take children
> from parents and into care. You don't have to take an anti-
> social work stance to be aware of how some of the functions
> of social work reproduce and reinforce institutional racism.
> (Roy, 1988, p. 209)

More specifically, black children have faced racism in the care system over a period of 30 years (Barnardos, 1966; Fitzherbert, 1967; Cheetham, 1981; Small, 1983; Ahmed, 1990a; Macdonald, 1992). Research has also shown that black children are more likely to be taken into care than white children, and when in care are more likely to be placed in residential homes than in foster care (Rowe and Lambert, 1970). Small has argued that white people take away black children as an indication and exercise of power which is why white children are not placed with black families. He calls this a 'one-way traffic' of black children to white families (Small, 1983).

Is this still the case ten years on? On the surface it appears that black people have been integrated into the child care system as a result of equal opportunities policies and training in awareness of race issues. In addition, the number of black social workers employed by social services departments has increased in the inner cities. Yet black children are still more likely to be taken into care. Section 71 of the Children Act 1989 specifically refers to the needs of black children and states that a child's religion, language and cultural needs should be met by the local authorities. Yet as Dutt (1991) argues, legislation and equal opportunities policies have led to no significant changes in service provision for black children. Although some of the policy arguments seem to be gaining ground, their actual impact remains minimal.

There appear to be three major reasons for the continuation of racist child care. First, there is a tendency to pathologise the black family. It is perceived as being problematic, and is considered to be inadequate in terms of providing black children with appropriate child care. In fact, as Small (1983) has pointed out, it is not the inadequacy of black parents that tends to determine who cares for black children in care but the power relations in society. Invariably there are widespread negative images of black parents which influence decisions made by white workers about child care. Furthermore, social work training does not prepare students to work through their often negative images of black people. Rather it tends to reinforce their prejudices (Katz, 1990).

Secondly, there is a lack of knowledge and understanding of the importance for a black child to have a positive black identity of her/himself. This has been highlighted by several writers and most effectively by Maxime (1986) in a child image of her/himself. In its simplest form it is the black child looking in a mirror – and seeing a blank. A positive sense of identity not only includes a mirror image but provides roots and a tradition for a child.

At a conference on black children in care a speaker put it eloquently when she said that without roots a tree dies, and indeed in a metaphoric sense so does the child. Perita Harris has argued that the likelihood of children in care entering psychiatric institutions is high:

> I'd like to quote you a letter I received this week from a young woman who's left care, aged 21, and living in London:

'I've been in care since I was five, fostered by many white families. I guess I wasn't treated any different by the parents. By the time I was nine, I noticed that I didn't have blond hair or blue eyes and white skin, in fact I noticed so much that I used to scrub my skin with a scourer in the bath, wishing and hoping I'd get lighter. I ended up with scars all over me. Then in my teens I took up scratching my skin on my arms every time I thought of my blackness, until I bled. I hated myself so much. After that, after going through my last school years as anorexia nervosa, I took up overdosing and spent the night every two or three months in hospital.' (Harris, 1991)

In discussions of identity and issues of child care practices it is all too easy to forget the human cost of bad practice. The 'Black and in Care' groups which I discuss later began in London and have evolved to support and advocate for black children in care. Unfortunately in practice a child's racial identity is rarely considered – beyond hair care, music and food. For the Black and in Care group the wider issues around providing a positive black environment for black children in care are of paramount importance.

Thirdly, assessments made by white social workers are often inadequate and ineffective (Small, 1983; Ahmed, 1993). Assessments of child care are based on Eurocentric models of families and have a value base which does not apply to black families (Joseph, Reddy and Chatterjee, 1990). So when white social workers are faced with having to undertake child protective investigations they are often ill-equipped to do so.

The major differences are that white values of individualism cannot be applied effectively to black families. Cannan (1983) pointed this out ten years ago and yet it is still evident in the practices of local authorities. She argued:

> the notion of individual self-fulfilment does not mesh with Indian (in my view black) views of the individual as part of a family . . . the western type self-determination can be damaging and undermining. (Cannan, 1983, p. 168)

Until white workers become competent in addressing fundamental differences such as these, there cannot be effective anti-racist social work. It is imperative that at each stage in the process of assessment of a black child or family there is constant questioning of the practices of those involved. In the liberal framework of the social services departments this is problematic due to the defensive nature of white workers when dealing with black families, together with a refusal to accept limitations of cultural perspectives in making assessments of black families (Dominelli, 1988).

Black Community Development Responses

During the 1980s black social workers began to look to black communities for responses to various issues. This alliance became an essential survival mechanism for the social workers. The concept of collective responsibility is one that can be traced back to the differences between the perception of the child as an individual and, in black cultures, as part of a whole community and family group (Brother Koka, 1991).

Throughout the encounter between black and white people, and through colonialism, the natural lifestyles of black families have been suppressed and a systematic Europeanisation of black peoples has been attempted. Historically, 'Natives had to undergo a Europeanisation process' (Chinweizu, 1975). In response to this black people have been active in protecting and mobilising in order to care for their children themselves. It is not evident in the literature how black people have come together in order to ensure that, once their children are taken in care, they are cared for by black families. There are two pertinent themes here: first, attempts by black people to reclaim their children; and second, attempts by institutions to prevent them from doing so. The latter has tended to be fairly subtle.

Black communities do not perceive their children to be the sole responsibility of natural parents. Many different patterns exist for the care of young children and most of these are based on the rearing of a child as part of a family and community. (Cannan, 1983; Joseph, Reddy and Chatterjee 1990). Carers form a wide group of adults with whom the child becomes familiar – extended families and maternal carers, for example. These patterns are entrenched in the deep-rooted ideology of 'collective responsibility'.

Community campaigns have been in evidence since the 'soul kids' campaign in 1973. This involved black women reaching out to the children and ensuring that social services made black families available to foster and adopt black children in care. In 1983 ABSWAP (Association of Black Social Workers and Allied Professions) argued to a House of Commons Select Committee that black children should not be placed with white families. Weise (1988) argued that black families are better equipped to provide black children with a positive identity to combat racism. Recent efforts have been made by the Black and in Care groups to ensure that resources are directed to black communities. As a result there have been campaigns by black workers to recruit black people to foster and adopt black children in care.

Black communities in Britain have been communities of resistance. Sivanandan (1990) has argued that social services departments, as well as the professionalisation of black people, have led to the demise or slow erosion of supportive networks in black communities. Yet, solidarity is a phenomenon of the resistance of black communities against racism. It is this aspect of communities which, if nurtured and developed, can be of lasting benefit to child care provision for black communities. This presents a dilemma: is it feasible to add to the already heavy burden on black people living in Britain today? Or should social services departments be compelled to provide the care required? The ideal would be for social services departments to support black family structures.

The examples below highlight attempts to change practice in the social services, including meetings at the highest level with the members of the department concerned. Black and in Care is a national voluntary organisation with groups in London, Manchester, Liverpool and Leicester. The group is unresourced nationally and is developed and maintained by committed black people. These include black professionals working with children as well as other people in black communities. It is a group which survives on networking.

The Leicester Black and in Care group came about as a result of frustrations felt by black workers at the treatment of black children in care. They built alliances with black community groups in order to devise a three stage-strategy:

- To provide information for black communities on the plight of black children in care – in general black communities are unaware about the situation of black children in care. This process was begun by students on placement organising an open day.
- To ensure that social services policies on child care include the rights of black children in care.

- To ensure that there are community-based initiatives which support black parents, especially black mothers, through an Asian mothers group.

The Leicester group has developed methods of working with issues of child care, including incorporating black community development issues as a theme; networking; and attempting to devise alternative ways of responding to needs.

In Southwark a black consortium met with the director of social services. The aim was to work together for policy development as well as to change individual clients' experiences of receiving social work support. The work has been perceived as successful both by the director concerned and by the black group involved in meeting him. Reasons cited for this success are that both parties had their own agendas and that the black group worked closely with the communities as well as black workers in the social services department. Furthermore, the huge gap that exists between black communities and the social services department was addressed by having direct discussions with decision makers. It is evident that such an effort required risk taking on the part of the director in Southwark. The success of the project relied solely on the relationship between the black and white representatives at the meetings. An honest and frank exchange of views led to innovative changes. The problems surrounding lack of resources to the authority were discussed with the director and, when it was shown that inadequate services were provided to the black communities, some resources were allocated to them.

The Leicester group had been in touch with the Southwark group through the National Black Caucus and attempted to have a similar dialogue with Leicestershire Social Services Department. In order to ensure that the group was in touch with national developments in the social work field, the Race Equality Unit at the National Institute for Social Work became involved. However, after a couple of meetings, Leicestershire declined to continue to meet with the group, arguing that it was not representative of local communities. The Leicestershire experience is not unique. Dialogue between local authorities and black communities has always been problematic.

When the meetings ceased the group decided to rethink the direction of its work. At the time the Children Act 1989 was about to be implemented and the group felt that the community needed to be informed of the Act's implications for them. A conference was duly organised. There were several speakers including Keith Vaz the local MP, local councillors, members of NISW's Race Equality Unit and Black and in Care representatives from London. The success of the day was dependent on the goodwill of the black voluntary sector and black individuals in the community. It was not resourced by the social services department. Organisers met with considerable institutional racism. They had asked social services for the day to be resourced but did not receive a response until two weeks before the event, by which time local black people had provided the majority of the resources needed. This self-organisation of black communities is an aspect of black community development which has sustained it in hostile political climates.

Students on placement supported the work of the group, as did a steering group made up of interested individuals and supporters. The steering group felt that in order to work effectively with local communities several levels of community involvement were required. It decided that until funds for work were forthcoming, and the black voluntary sector and individual black people were not having to compensate for social services, it would concentrate on supporting individual cases – either families or children in care. The group had come to the conclusion that working with the social services department was not a constructive use of its time and energies. It was considered more useful to support individual families facing difficulties so that they could have some tangible support.

Individual Case Work: Two Examples

Ms A came from a small and remote part of India. She spoke a dialect of Punjabi. She had come to England to join her husband who had been labelled mentally ill. Ms A gave birth to her child and because she did not respond to the child as was expected she had been moved to a psychiatric institution soon after the birth.

This event traumatised her and she was in shock for a long time. Asian women in her position would normally have received considerable support from the family, but in Ms A's case they were all in India. Soon after Ms A left hospital there was a suspected child abuse investigation. A case conference was held. The consultant argued that the child had been shaken and had received head injuries. Both baby and the couple's other child, a two-year-old, were taken into care immediately after the conference. However, the Asian woman social worker abstained from the decision as she felt that the evidence was not conclusive.

The Black and in Care group was asked by the family for support and an assessment was made from a black perspective. This argued that the family had been systematically mistreated and misunderstood by the health care system (the psychiatric assessments seemed to have completely misdiagnosed Ms A as being mentally ill). The major difficulty was that the family's lifestyle and culture was very different from the local Asian community in Leicester. The family had no means of support from anywhere.

The 'abuse' was later checked by an Asian consultant who questioned the medical grounds on which the suspicion was based. He argued that the damage could have been caused by a rare bone complaint which might make the child weak. The children had been placed in care with white foster parents and the two-year-old showed signs of distress by hitting his head on the wall. The group befriended the parents. Members explained the system and what was going on. They visited regularly and provided them with support. The husband's mother was brought over from India to support the mother in child caring. Immigration advisors were used to help with the process. The children were placed in the positive environment of a family centre, and an Asian social worker was allocated. By working with the community and pressing for black workers the group argued successfully for the children to be returned home.

X was a victim of sexual abuse by a white man and black woman. At the age of eight he was beginning to show signs of disturbed behaviour, especially towards men. He was taken into care because his mother could no longer cope with him. He was placed in a residential home for older boys, especially juvenile offenders – an inappropriate environment for him. The group went to a case meeting where a discussion took place about the child's behaviour and how it could be addressed.

Due to the severity of the child's distress, an assessment was made by the group that the child required specialist black counselling. Although members of the group included qualified counsellors the group thought that this child required a black psychiatrist. The group made their assessment and argued that in order to help the child the social services department would have to pay for specialist help. The department did not respond by allocating the appropriate finances. Over a period of time the group remained in contact with the child. He was invited to attend a funday for black children in care. He continued to be disruptive but he made good use of the black environment provided by the group.

In most cases where the groups have attempted to support black children in care there have been problems of resources and access. Working in partnership with local authorities has proved to be difficult in practice.

Asian Women's Group

These frustrations led to the setting up of an Asian women's group in Leicester. An Asian woman student on placement with the social services department undertook the development work as a result of a case concerning an Asian child who was failing to thrive. The child's mother had been receiving support from a white health visitor and a white social worker. She had recently arrived from India to marry her husband and had been ill after the birth of her daughter. She faced isolation in a white working-class council estate. Her health visitor had provided her with dietary information which she had not read, first, because the material was not given to her in a language she could read, and secondly because the dietary information was totally inappropriate for her. The woman had been seen by her social worker on one occasion. The child's development was of concern to the department, and both the social worker and the health visitor agreed that the child was failing to thrive. The case raised issues about the centile charts used by health visitors to assess Asian children.

Young and Connelly (1981) found that Asian women workers were far better equipped than their white colleagues to support Asian women clients. This was particularly due to language skills and an understanding of family structures. In this instance the worker was able to establish that a mother-in-law would ensure that not only this woman but also other young mothers in the area would be in touch with an older figure who would provide necessary information about child care – information which was not Eurocentric.

The group was set up by networking with Asian women in the city. With the support of a women's centre and an Asian woman development worker from the city council, the group began to meet. This networking provides a valuable example of neighbourhood and interest networking which proved to be essential for the development of this group. Discussions were held on an informal basis with the new mothers and the older women, who advised the younger mothers on child care issues in a culturally appropriate manner. The setting was informal.

The work was invaluable for a number of reasons but primarily because the reasoning behind it was to ensure that the advice was based on the mother's own viewpoint. The principle of collective responsibility was highlighted by the way in which the older women supported the younger mothers. The group helped to reduce isolation for all the women who attended the group. It made older women feel supportive and provided them with a social outlet. The initiative led to a more effective response and empowered the women, who later went on to develop a group for activities and outings.

In developing such projects there are several issues which need to be borne in mind. First, there is no substitute for statutory and well-resourced input for black communities in child care support. However, it is partly due to the lack of such facilities that black people have organised in order to respond to their own needs. Moreover, such examples indicate how much the statutory services need to develop their anti-racist practices before they are accessible to black people in any meaningful manner. In a similar discussion Ahmed (1990a) argues that self-help is no substitute for the work that is allocated to local authorities by legislation. The contract culture induced by the Community Care and Children Acts, and partnerships with non-profit making organisations, allow this to be developed further. Nevertheless local authorities tend to overlook black projects and to fund larger white organisations who have included in their bids work with black people. This repeats the inequality that exists in local authorities.

Conclusion

I have attempted to identify some of the principles that guide black community development and child care. The chapter has focused directly on the issues pertinent to black community development and by definition this differs from the community development which comes from the dominant culture. The major task of black community development is not only to address racism and racist practices in all areas of black people's lives, but to develop communities through black self-organisation to meet the needs of black communities. Black children in care pose a particular challenge to black community development as a group within but taken out of the community, and as a result of the problems faced by black parents. I have argued that as long as black people within the social work system work with black communities in a positive manner the outcomes can be effective.

The chapter has highlighted the importance of the four major themes in black community development: networking; challenging racism; developing alternatives; and working with the principle of collective responsibility. The networking approach in particular has led to some successful outcomes: the Asian women's group, the Black and in Care groups, the development of information to black communities through black community care projects, etc. All these have been successful not for the meagre sums that might have been allocated to them but for the commitment and the initiatives employed. The only successes that the group has met with are those where it has mobilised the black community. This has included a national dimension through the Southwark black consortium and NISW's black workers, in addition to the local Asian women's organisations and support from black workers in the social services departments.

Although agencies have statutory duties to work with black children they fail to do so in a way that develops the children as positive members of British society. The treatment of black children in care has outraged black communities, which is why they have been active in working to challenge discriminatory behaviour. There is a great deal of evidence to suggest that social services fail black children. The community development approach signals a new way forward in providing child care services to black communities. Could this finally mean that black children, through effective and well-resourced black community development services, receive the services that they deserve?

References

Ahmed, S. (1990) *Practice with Care*, London: NISW Race Equality Unit.

Ahmed, S. (1990a) 'Translating Race Equality Policies into Practice' in *Critical Social Policy*, no. 27.

Ahmed, S. (1993) *Social Work With Black Children and their Families*, London: Batsford.

Association of Black Social Workers and Allied Professions (1983) *Black Children in Care: Evidence to the House of Commons Social Services Departments and 'Ethnic Minorities'*, London: ABSWAP.

Atkin, K. (1991) 'In a Multicultural Society: Incorporating the View of Policy and Politics' in *Community Care*, vol. 19, no. 3, pp. 159–66.

Barnardos Working Party (1966) *Racial Integration and Barnardos Homes*, London: Barnardos.

Brother Koka (1991) 'Collective Responsibility in Child Care' in *Black Children in Care*, Conference Report, Leicester.

Cannan, C. (1983) 'Social Work, Race Relations and the Social Work Curriculum' in *New Community*, vol. IX, nos. 1/2, autumn/winter.

Cheetham, J. (1981) *Social and Community Work in a Multi-Racial Society*, New York: Harper and Row.

Chinweizu (1975) *The West and the Rest of Us*, New York: Vintage Books.

Commission for Racial Equality/Association of Directors of Social Services (1978) *Multi-cultural Britain: The Social Services Response*, London: CRE/ADSS.

Dominelli, L. (1988) *Anti-racist Social Work*, London: MacMillan/BASW.

Dutt, R. (1991) 'A Historical and Policy Perspective' in *Black Children in Care*, Conference Report, Leicester.

Fitzherbert, K. (1967) *West Indian Children in London*, London: Bell and Sons.

Harris, A. (1991) *Black Children in Care*, Conference Report, Leicester.

Joseph, G., Reddy, V. and Chatterjee, M. (1990) 'Eurocentratricism in the Social Sciences' in *Race and Class*, no. 31(4).

Katz, J.H. (1990) *White Awareness Handbook for Race Awareness Training*, USA: University of Oklahoma.

Macdonald, S. (1992) *All Equal under the Act*, London: Race Equality Unit, National Institute of Social Work.

Maxime, J. (1986) 'Some Psychological Models of Black Self Concept' in *Social Work with Black Families and Children*, ed. S. Ahmed, J. Cheetham and J. Small London: Batsford.

Rowe, J. and Lambert, L. (1970) *Children Who Wait*, London: Routledge and Keegan Paul.

Roy, P. (1988) 'Social Services' in *Britain's Black Population: A New Perspective*, 2nd edition, ed. A. Bhat, R. Carr-Hill and S. Ohri, The Radical Statistics Group, London: Gower.

Sivanandan, A. (1990) *Black Communities Care Project*, Conference Report, London: NISW.

Small, J. (1983) in *Social Work with Black Children and their Families*, eds. S. Ahmed, J. Cheetham and J. Small, London: Batsford.

Weise, J. (1988) 'Transracial Adoption' in *Social Work Monograph 60*, Norwich: University of East Anglia.

Young, K. and Connelly, N. (1981) *Policy and Practice in the Multiracial City*, London: Policy Studies Institute.

3 Children and Young People – Disadvantage, Community and the Children Act 1989

Teresa Smith

Introduction

This book is about children's experiences – growing up, as young adults, as members of their families and communities and as individuals. How can we describe that experience, set it in a policy context, and evaluate the impact of policies on it?

Bruner, the American psychologist, began his review of family policy and the under fives at the beginning of the 1980s thus:

> Every nation, implicity or explicitly, has a policy towards its children. If it is pluralistic and laissez-faire as it has been idealised in the liberal ideology of the West, it is nonetheless a policy and it has its effects . . . It consists of many kinds of decisions: some have to do with 'safety net' provisions for children and families in poverty, in trouble, or otherwise at risk – the social services; others have to do with the provision of educational opportunity and the cultivation of human resources – the educational services. (Bruner, 1980, p. 1)

Is policy towards children and families as fragmented in the early 1990s as it was a decade ago, with socialisation and child care still largely a private matter within the family? The notion of a 'child impact' scrutiny of new legislation to check for its implications for the lives of children – environmental, educational, social, health – has been much discussed but never implemented: a powerful example is the outline of children's participation and rights published by the Children's Legal Centre (1993) as its 'agenda for the future'. Yet there have been two developments within the last few years which should offer hope.

First, children and young people have begun to be seen as individuals with views that should be listened to, with rights to make their own decisions, a principle encapsulated in the Children Act 1989 and by the UK ratification in December 1991 of the UN Convention on the Rights of the Child. Children's rights are at least on the agenda.

But it is largely uncharted territory, despite the arguments for a children's rights commissioner (Rosenbaum and Newell, 1991), the establishment of the Children's Rights Development Unit, and a handful of legal cases concerning the rights of young people to make decisions about which parent they wish to live with.

Second, the Children Act 1989, in bringing together previous legislation regarding children and young people and their families, has been hailed as 'undoubtedly one of the most radical and far-reaching reforms of the private and public law affecting children' (Bainham, 1991, p. 1) – although it is worth noting that it does not refer to children's 'rights' and in this respect is more limited than the UN Convention. Yet, at the same time, the disadvantages faced by many children and young people are increasingly in the public eye.

This chapter asks whether the notion of collective action by or on behalf of children and young people is a reality, and whether the new legislation is likely to support and promote such action to improve their life chances. But first we consider the evidence concerning the disadvantages facing children and young people today.

Children, Young People and Disadvantage

There is a groundswell of concern about children in Britain growing up in poor and disadvantaged families. Official statistics, research studies, and surveys combine to document the increase in low incomes, homelessness and unemployment experienced by children in their families and by young people directly.

Children are profoundly affected by their family circumstances – by illness, poverty, poor housing. The numbers of children and young people in the poorest families are increasing rapidly. In 1979, 1.4 million dependent children were living in households with incomes below half the national average; in 1990/91 the figure was 3.9 million, an increase from one-tenth to one-third of the age group (Department of Social Security, 1993). Average incomes, while rising for the population as a whole, have fallen for the groups at the bottom, including lone parents and unemployed people. In 1979, 28 per cent dependent children with a lone parent were living in families with incomes below half the national average; by 1990/91, the figure was 74 per cent. At the same time there is increasing evidence associating poor child health and greater mortality with poverty and deprivation (Seymour, 1992).

The massive increase in 16-year-olds staying in full-time education (from 38 per cent in 1979/80 to 66 per cent in 1991/2) hides alarming statistics on unemployment among young people. In January 1993, one million 16- to 24-year-olds were unemployed – one in six of the age group. Over 100,000 of these were under 18. These figures conceal striking differences between ethnic groups. In summer 1992, when average unemployment was 10 per cent, the figure for 16- to 19-year-olds was 21 per cent – but while the average for white young people was 20 per cent, that for non-whites was double this, at 42 per cent (Taylor, 1993). Even this figure masks considerably higher rates for some groups, for example West Indian/Guyanese young people.

The complexity of the benefits system for young people has been well documented. Since September 1988 most 16- and 17-year-olds not in work or full-time education have not been entitled to welfare benefits. Instead, they have been guaranteed a place on Youth Training with a training allowance. At the same time, discretionary short-term payments of Income Support were introduced for young people in danger of 'severe hardship'. But reports on the Youth Training programme (Maclagan, 1992; Chatrik and de Sousa, 1993) demonstrate that there are too few places to meet the need – particularly for black and ethnic minority young people.

The exclusion of many 16- and 17-year-olds from benefit has sharply increased the numbers of homeless young people. Shelter estimated in 1990 that there were 150,000 homeless young people in Britain, 50,000 of them in London. Their own stories illustrate vividly the pressures on such young people, facing threats or overcrowding at home and hostility as 'layabouts' on the streets, with unsuitable or no accommodation (Barnardo's, 1988). In Centrepoint's 1989 survey in London 80 per cent of the young people interviewed talked about eviction or family arguments as the main reason for leaving their last home; only 16 per cent gave more hopeful reasons such as looking for a job or following up offers. Many came from highly disadvantaged circumstances: 41 per cent had lived in a children's home at some stage, 16 per cent with foster parents, 49 per cent in a squat, and 78 per cent had slept rough (Randall, 1989). Homeless young people include groups that are particularly vulnerable to discrimination and exploitation, such as young women, young black people and runaways.

What of young people, and their families, who come to the attention of social services departments? Research demonstrates the importance of preventive services offering support and practical resources (Gibbons, 1990). 'Children in need' are not characteristically children with 'abusive or neglectful' parents. The clearest evidence on the link between disadvantage and what might be seen as 'the heavy end' of social services departments' statutory responsibilities – reception of children into care – comes from a study carried out by Bebbington and Miles (1989). This work demonstrates vividly the relative chances of children and young people from different circumstances and backgrounds coming to the attention of the social services departments. Briefly, the child of a white, two-parent family not dependent on benefits, with three or fewer children, living in an owner-occupied house with more rooms than people, has a one in 7,000 chance of being taken into care. In contrast, as Kanchan Jadeja shows in Chapter 2 above, a child of mixed ethnic origin, with a lone parent dependent on benefits, four or more children in the family, living in privately rented accommodation with more people than rooms, has a one in ten chance of being taken into care. These findings do not mean that poor families are necessarily poor at looking after their children, but they are starkly suggestive of the pressures on disadvantaged families.

The picture presented so far is one of a substantial group of children in poor and disadvantaged families, and unemployed and homeless young people for whom even a residual 'safety net' role of the state is clearly ineffective. The processes at work are those of racism, poverty, disadvantage and powerlessness. What can be done? This chapter attempts to link three themes: first, children and young people as 'active learners/active participants' in their families and neighbourhoods; second, current ideas about 'empowerment', 'participation', and 'consultation', and their application to children and young people; and third, collective approaches to children's and young people's issues and the Children Act 1989.

The Child as 'Active Learner'/'Active Participant'?

'Listening to the client' may not be the revolutionary departure it was in the days of *The Client Speaks* (Mayer and Timms, 1970), when 'the consumer viewpoint' was merely taken as a symptom of the underlying problem, but young people with voices and decisions of their own have only recently been acknowledged. In much of the literature on homelessness it is the voices of the young people themselves that we hear.

The idea of the pre-school child as 'active learner' has a long history. Children and parents as partners in a process of 'active learning' is a familiar theme in pre-school and community education and research, even if central government in the 1980s and 1990s has been more concerned with education of the statutory age group and the relationship between the education system and the labour market. However, pre-school provision is once again on the official agenda – partly as a result of a 'law and order' interest in evidence that pre-school programmes can be effective at producing law-abiding adolescents, 'active learners' throughout their school careers, motivated and skilled to enter the labour market (Schweinhart and Weikart, 1993). This is demonstrated by the Home Office's sponsorship of pre-school projects in inner-city areas, and publications on parenting and delinquency such as *Crime and the Family* (Utting et al., 1993) which argue for a range of family support schemes, pre-school provision and school- and community-based interventions to provide resources and skills for families in disadvantaged areas.

But what is it in these schemes that 'works'? Children in the High/Scope programmes sponsored by the Home Office are expected to control their own learning, to decide their own activity for the day, plan how to do it, and report back on what they have achieved. This is Bruner's 'active learner'. The justification of this approach is that the child's understanding and motivation is increased. The child learns more powerfully from internalising the process. There is a positive interaction between child and family, between home and school or pre-school, and a 'positive cycle' is established which takes into account the child's and adult's motivation and attitudes as well as the child's understanding:

> It seems possible that mutual reinforcement processes occurred between the early education participants and their parents. Perhaps the children's participation in a programme raised the mother's hopes and expectations for their children . . . mothers of early education participants continued to have higher aspirations for their children than the children had for themselves and thus presumably exerted more pressure to achieve . . . parents of the programme group reported more satisfaction with their children's schoolwork . . . Perhaps children interpreted these parental attitudes as a belief in and support of their efforts, and it served to spur them on. (Lazar and Darlington, 1982, p. 63)

How can this be applied to young adults? Perhaps the nearest equivalent to Bruner's pre-school 'active learner' is to be found in the youth work curriculum set out by the Youth Service, defined by the Education Minister Alan Howarth as a framework for young people that should 'empower them to understand and act on the personal, social and political issues which affect their lives' (quoted in *Youth Social Work*, winter 1990–91, 2, 4). Youth social work or social action typically deals with issues such as homelessness, drugs, poverty, offending and how young people can acquire some power over their lives. Young people's organisations such as the National Association of Young People in Care (NAYPIC) and projects such as Save the Children's Lifechance are examples. Here the notion of 'active learner' has to be understood with notions such as 'empowerment' and 'participation'. Kanchan Jadeja's discussion in Chapter 2 above on Black and In Care groups speaks to these themes too.

Empowerment, Participation, Consultation and Partnership

Like the 'active learner', the concept of participation has a long pedigree, and one that draws on different traditions. From the 1960s onwards, the push to involve parents in their children's education has roots in demonstrating the effect of parental participation on young children's development. Debate in the 1960s and 1970s defined 'involvement' largely as 'better informed' – parents were to have more information about school activities, and were to be brought into the classroom in order to learn more about the school curriculum and appropriate methods of teaching young children, while teachers would learn more about the home background of their pupils. 'Participation' for community groups and community activists in the 1960s and 1970s had its roots in political theory analysis of power (Lukes, 1974): who controls decisions about resources and over issues such as the lack of playspace or decent housing, the redevelopment of inner-city slums, the building of new motorways? 'Active citizenship' and the 'Citizen's Charter' in the 1980s and 1990s draws on notions of the rights and duties of citizenship and 'consumer involvement'. People who use services have the right to be consulted about their planning and delivery (Croft and Beresford, 1990). Parents should control school governing bodies; patients should choose the best health care through the free market.

But are these labels interchangeable, or do they conceal – or reveal – different nuances, different and potentially conflicting traditions? The question is what is seen as the problem. Trends over the last ten years show two separate developments (Smith, 1989). The first can be illustrated by the conflict in the 1980s between managerial and political initiatives to develop participatory structures in local authority services. Moves to 'decentralise' 'patch'-based offices in social services departments were on the whole initiated 'top-down' by managers – the problem was defined as one of communication, which could be improved by local offices, user groups in establishments like children's homes or family centres, more consultation, more opportunities for officers and local authority members to hear what local people had to say before decisions were taken. The second can be illustrated by moves, particularly in Labour councils, to 'democratise' services by decentralising political decision-making to the neighbourhood level – the problem here was defined as one essentially of the relationship between the individual and the state, and the individual's lack of power in this relationship.

'Decentralisation' and 'patch' are not currently fashionable. But the questions raised in the 1980s by these developments are still real. What part do people, young or old, play in determining the shape of their communities and their services? The critique of public sector services can take two forms (Hoggett and Hambleton, 1987). One is essentially administrative, managerial and 'consumerist': reforming the organisation can improve efficiency and responsiveness to the consumer. The other is essentially political and 'collectivist': the emphasis is on changing the relationship between services and consumers by 'democratising' the service – that is, changing the power relationship. A similar conflict can be seen in different efforts to involve people in social services: 'consumerism' means information seeking and consultation, whereas 'self-advocacy' aims for empowerment with people speaking up for themselves and attempting to gain greater control. The former is service or provider led, the latter user led.

The implication of this distinction is as follows. The 'consumerist' approach is essentially individualistic. Responsiveness is to the individual, with systems for individual complaints, and carefully constructed packages of individual treatment or care. This approach is compatible with a community social work style, with close attention paid to community resources, community networks and the voluntary sector to support vulnerable individuals and families. The 'collectivist' approach, on the other hand, is essentially a collective analysis of issues and strategies, and the playing out of these in and by groups, networks, organisations and neighbourhoods. Community care, or community social work with its starting point in concern for the individual in the community, has to be underpinned by an understanding of how communities and organisations work and can be fostered. This, in short, requires community work skills and knowledge.

'Empowerment' literally means the giving of power. It thus requires an analysis of a relationship in which one party has power and relinquishes (all or some of) it, while the other has no power but acquires it. 'Partnership' implies a relationship in which two parties have equal power. Some commentators have argued that while social workers can *empower* clients, there can be no *partnership* between client and social worker in a statutory relationship. Whether or not there can be partnership between large statutory social services departments and small voluntary organisations or community groups is also debatable.

What are the implications of this debate for young people? The clear intention of those who framed the Children Act 1989 was to empower children and young people and enable their voices to be heard. Organisations committed to children's rights, such as the Children's Legal Centre and the Children's Rights Development Unit, are important. So is the growing determination of many professionals to consult young people – examples at different levels include individual social workers making sure young people are present at care reviews, and umbrella organisations such as the Coalition on Young People and Social Security (COYPSS) drawing attention to the inadequacies of current benefits and training policies. Most important of all, however, is the emergence of self-advocacy groups of young people.

But there may be difficulties for a group stigmatised as 'clients' in winning public credibility and access to decision making on their own terms rather than simply 'token participation'. As Arnstein wrote in 1969:

> Participation without redistribution of power is an empty and frustrating process for the powerless. It allows policy-holders to claim that all sides were considered but makes it possible for only some of those sides to benefit. It maintains the status quo. (Arnstein (1969) quoted in Hallett, 1987)

Arnstein's 'ladder of participation' has been usefully adapted as a metaphor to describe eight levels of young people's participation in projects (Flekkoy quoted in Franklin, 1992):

1. Manipulation: children do or say what adults suggest they do, but have no real understanding of the issues; or children are asked what they think, adults use some of the ideas but do not tell them what influence they have had on the final decision.
2. Decoration: children take part in an event, e.g. by singing, dancing, or wearing T-shirts with logos on, but they do not really understand the issues.
3. Tokenism: children are asked to say what they think about an issue but have little or no choice about the way they express those views or the scope of the ideas they can express.
4. Assigned but informed: adults decide on the project and children volunteer for it. The children understand the project, and know who decided why they should be involved and why. Adults respect their views.
5. Consulted and informed: the project is designed and run by adults but children are consulted. They have a full understanding of the process and their opinions are taken seriously.
6. Adult initiated, shared decisions with children: adults have the initial idea but children are involved in every step of the planning and implementation. Not only are their views considered, but they are also involved in taking the decisions.

7. Child initiated and directed: children have the initial idea and decide how the project is to be carried out. Adults are available but do not take charge.
8. Child initiated, shared decisions with adults: children have the ideas, set up the project and come to adults for advice, discussion and support. The adults do not direct but offer their expertise for children to consider.

Flekkoy suggested that only the last five levels should be considered as participation – just as Arnstein argued that her first five levels were non-participation or degrees of tokenism, and only the last three were degrees of real power. Flekkoy continued thus:

> On whatever level children and young people have such opportunities – which can be useful learning opportunities, to learn what the consequences of voicing opinions or voting are – it must be made very clear, to them as well as to anybody else, when they can actually make a decision which will be followed through, and when their opinions are, like anybody else's, subject to decision by and through a democratic process. If they are led to believe that their opinions carry more weight than they actually do, children and young people, like adults, will either give up trying or become rebellious.

This is a classic statement both of community organisation applied to young people – learning how to organise groups and make decisions – and of the 'active learning'/'active participation' discussed in the previous section.

'Putting the community' into the Children Act 1989

Community work round children's issues was a major activity in the 1960s and 1970s – for example, community action campaigns round playspace and playgroups. There are still many examples of small community groups setting up – toddler groups, Saturday schools, adventure playgrounds. But funding and recognition is much more difficult to get as local authority funding is squeezed, and national funding such as the Urban Programme has cut support for playschemes and holiday schemes. In addition, funding for the youth services has been cut – according to estimates by the National Youth Agency, in 62 per cent of local authorities' budgets for 1993/94 alone. The shift to 'purchaser/provider' arrangements in social services departments and 'service agreements' with voluntary organisations may penalise small autonomous groups. Statutory pressures mean that work on issues other than those which can easily be subsumed under a 'statutory' or 'social work relevant' heading are likely to be ignored. Connections are often not recognised – or, if recognised, work is not funded – between unemployment, health or play projects and their impact on life chances for children and young people.

Collective approaches and community action on children's and young people's issues is just as important in the 1990s, and must be embedded in mainstream social services if recent legislation like the Children Act 1989 is to be properly implemented. At first sight it may seem odd to link community work with the Children Act. In *Putting the Community into Community Care*, Armstrong and Henderson (1992) point out that community workers have for a long time neglected social welfare as a 'soft' issue, unlike 'hard' issues such as housing and employment. The same point might be made about child care. There is no mention of 'the community' or of 'community work' in the Children Act, or in the volumes of guidance published by the Department of Health. Yet there is an ethos throughout the Act of keeping children within their families in the community wherever possible, and taking the child's own views into account, and an emphasis on openness, information, consultation, partnership. All of this may be described as no more than current 'good practice'. But an understanding of community and the principles and practice of community work are essential to this 'good practice' in two ways.

First, 'participation' and the 'collective approach' are critical concepts in community work. This means helping people to define issues not as individual but as collective problems, and to think through strategies for tackling inequalities. It also means helping people to recognise issues to do with power and powerlessness and to fight for their rights. If we apply this to children and young people, we can recognise the importance of self-advocacy groups, organisations committed to a 'rights approach', and the growing acceptance of consulting children and young people in decisions on their own futures.

Second, research on informal networks and community reveals the importance of kinship, workplace, religious and ethnic affiliations as the basis for caring relationships, and of common issues as a basis for common action. There is a wealth of literature on youth culture but little attempt to analyse this as a basis for common action or caring relationships. This work remains to be done.

How may we apply community work principles and concepts to work with children and young people?

1. Empowerment: the Children Act gives children and young people more say – for example, over where they live (section 20 (6 and 11). This requires information and advice, support networks, self-advocacy, and self-help and campaigning groups. This sort of work is beginning in the youth work field. Community workers have considerable experience of helping such developments with adults; their skills could be applied to young people's concerns.
2. Organising: self-advocacy and self-help groups recognise the importance of moving away from individually-based to community-based approaches. Young people's concerns are similar to those of adults – finding a job and somewhere to live, developing relationships with adults and their own age group, negotiating their way through the intricacies of bureaucracy. Young homeless people in Oxford developing a self-build co-operative scheme spoke of the power and confidence that grew out of being part of a group (Burke, 1993). Again, youth and community workers have experience of helping people to recognise collective concerns and develop the skills to organise collectively.
3. Lobbying and self-advocacy: young people, like adults, have the right to speak for themselves. Community workers have experience of helping people to learn the necessary skills, and of standing back to let them get on with it.
4. The importance of information: the Act requires (schedule 2, section 1) local authorities to 'take such steps as are reasonably practicable to ensure that those who might benefit from the services receive the information relevant to them'. Information, as any community worker knows, is most likely to be picked up and used in shops, pubs, post offices, launderettes, doctors' surgeries, particularly if it is in a form designed by local people themselves, not designed by bureaucrats and kept behind the desk in the town hall.

There is also an important debate about 'need'. The Children Act lays down the general duty of local authorities to provide support services for children and families. It states: 'It shall be the duty of every local authority to safeguard and promote the welfare of children within their area who are in need.' This requires authorities to identify 'children in need' (section 17), and to 'have regard to the different racial groups to which children in need belong' (schedule 2, section 11). How has this been interpreted by authorities in the definitions of 'children in need' they are required to publish? Department of Health guidelines (Department of Health, 1991, para. 2.4) make it clear that simply restricting the definition to children considered to be at risk or actually on the at risk register or already looked after by the authority would be contravening the Act. The ambiguities in the Act, and in the notion of 'prevention', have been described with various degrees of scepticism by commentators such as Packman and Jordan (1991). Studies of the first year of implementing the Act (Aldgate et al., 1993) show that children and young people 'in the community' receive a comparatively low priority rating unless they are thought to be at risk of significant harm or neglect, or are already in accommodation or care. Less than a third of the local authorities in the survey gave priority in their statements on 'children in need' to children or young people with health needs or disabilities, who were drug or solvent users, homeless or living in bed and breakfast accommodation, from poor families or with unemployed or lone parents.

We can see from the statistics quoted earlier that large numbers of children and young people are growing up in hardship. But current implementation of the Children Act suggests that many children and young people in extremely disadvantaged circumstances of poverty, homelessness and unemployment may not be recognised as 'in need'. This is a punitive situation for a most vulnerable age group.

Yet it is quite clear that the Children Act is *preventive in intention*. One of the legal commentaries on the Act states that:

> interpretations . . . are concerned as much (if not more) with prevention as they are with cure . . . the preventive duty . . . must be extracted from the definition of a child in need . . . the authority must concern itself not only with those children who are already suffering from a low standard of health or development but also with those who are likely to find themselves in this position unless the authority takes preventive action. (Bainham, 1991 p. 62)

As the National Council of Voluntary Child Care Organisations and Family Rights Group have argued, implementation of the Act should be based on values of universalism – that is, everyone should have rights to services of a universal kind as well as specialist services for particular difficulties; equality and equity of access to services without stigma; normality; and participation. These groups' working assumptions were that, as a general rule, people are competent, difficulties are structural, and needs should be defined in relation to services required rather than deficiencies.

For children and young people, this surely means that public services must pay attention to play in the neighbourhood – playgroups, space for parent and toddler meeting places in every street or block of flats, adventure playspace in every neighbourhood if not on every corner, youth clubs; to relevant information for young people that is accessible in form and location; to children's and young people's rights and to opportunities for organisation, self-help, campaigning and self-advocacy; to rights to decent housing, education, health and employment.

References

Aldgate, J., Tunstill, J. and McBeath, G. (1993) *National Monitoring of the Children Act: Part III s 17 – The First Year* in Secretaries of State for Health and for Wales (1993) *Children Act Report 1993,* London: HMSO.

Armstrong, J. and Henderson, P. (1992): *Putting the Community into Community Care*, London: Community Development Foundation.

Barnardo's (1988): *'Tell It As It Is': Young People And Homelessness*, Newcastle upon Tyne: Barnardo's.

Bainham, A. (1991): *Children – The New Law: the Children Act 1989*, Bristol: Jordan.

Bebbington, A. and Miles, J. (1989): 'The Background of Children who Enter Local Authority Care' *British Journal of Social Work*, 19 (5), 349–68.

Bruner, J. (1980): *Under Five in Britain* London: Grant McIntyre.

Burke, T. (1993): 'Building a Brighter Future' *Young People Now*, May, quoted in Children's Rights Development Unit (1993) *Briefing: the Rights of Children and Young People to a Safe, Healthy Environment: Consultation Document*, London: CRDU.

Chatrik, B. and de Sousa E. (1993): *Where Are They Now? Black Young People and the Youth Training Guarantee*, Black Employment and Training Forum. London: Runnymede Trust.

Children's Legal Centre (1993) 'Agenda for the Future' *Childright*, 100, October 1993, pp. 2–3.

Croft, S. and Beresford, P. (1990): *From Paternalism to Participation: Involving People in Social Services*, London: Open Services Project/Joseph Rowntree Foundation.

Department of Health (1991): *The Children Act 1989: guidance and Regulations. Volume 2: Family Support, Day Care and Educational Provision for Young Children*, London: HMSO.

Department of Social Security (1993): *Households Below Average Income: a Statistical Analysis 1979–1990/91*, London: HMSO.

Franklin, A. (1992) 'Children and Young People's Participation Rights', paper for Save the Children, September/October 1992.

Gibbons, J. (1990): *Family Support and Prevention: Studies in Local Areas*, London: HMSO/National Institute for Social Work.

Hallett, C. (1987) *Critical issues in participation*, Newcastle-upon-Tyne: Association of Community Workers.

Hoggett, P. and Hambleton, R. (1987) *Decentralising Democracy: Localising Public Services*, Bristol: School for Advanced Urban Studies. Occasional Paper 28.

Lazar, I. and Darlington, R. (1982) *Lasting Effects of Early Education: a Report from the Consortium for Longitudinal Studies*, Monographs of the Society for Research in Child Development, 195.

Lukes, S. (1974): *Power: A Radical View*, London: Macmillan.

Maclagan, E. (1992): *A Broken Promise: the Failure of Youth Training Policy*, London: Youthaid/COYPSS, Barnardos.

Mayer, J.E. and Timms, N. (1970): *The Client Speaks: Working Class Impressions of Casework*, London: Routledge & Kegan Paul.

Packman, J. and Jordon, B. (1991): 'The Children Act: Looking Forward, Looking Back' *British Journal of Social Work*, 21 (4), 315–27.

Randall, G. (1989): *Homeless and Hungry: a Sign of The Times*, London: Centrepoint Soho.

Rosenbaum, M. and Newell, P. (1991): *Taking Children Seriously: a Proposal for a Children's Rights Commissioner*, London: Calouste Gulbenkian Foundation.

Schweinhart, L. and Weikart, D. (1993): *Significant Benefits: the High/Scope Perry Preschool Study Through Age 27*, unpublished.

Seymour, J. (1992) *Give Us A Chance: Children, Poverty and the Health of the Nation*, London: Save the Children Fund.

Smith, T. (1989) 'Decentralisation and Community' *British Journal of Social Work*, 19, 137–48.

Taylor, D. (1993): 'Unemployment: Ethnic Minority Young People' *Youthaid Working Brief*, issue 44, May 1993, 9.

Utting, D. Bright, J. and Henricson, H. (1993): *Crime and the Family: Improving Childrearing and Preventing Delinquency*, London: Family Policy Studies Centre.

Youth Social Work, 2, winter 1990/91. Leicester: National Youth Bureau.

Part 2 Environment

Community development has been slow to engage with the 'green' environmental agenda – a contrast with its strong track record on the built environment and play. Yet there is a growing awareness among environmentalists of the need for stronger links between green and community issues. Roome (1993), in his analysis of green perspectives, underlines this point:

> There is an increasing recognition that environmental management and improvement is a participative exercise which involves discussion and transaction with local people. Environmental action is therefore increasingly bound up with community practice. (Roome, 1993, p. 205)

It is a safe bet that we will witness increasing commitment by community development in this vitally important area. Community development can provide methods and techniques to reach out to local people. Equally important, there is a natural consonance of values between community development and environmentalism – equal treatment for all, people-led policies, local control, participatory politics. Finally, community development is in a good position to make connections between aspects of community life that impact on people directly – poor quality housing, high unemployment, disillusionment with remote decision-making processes – and global environmental concerns. This could be a significant contribution to the process of environmental education. Arguably, regeneration policies and programmes are inseparable from the future of the environment. We are beginning to see this argument being made more strongly as well as exciting examples of practice in both the urban and rural contexts. It is possible to envisage a coalition here between children's rights advocates and regeneration experts around a shared agenda:

> Communities that are to be given new life by having children as their focus will have to give parents priority in local

71

housing too, and that means priority for the right housing
in the right place. (Leach, 1994, p. 263)

Yet the involvement of children in environmental issues is often
delicately poised. On the one hand no group has a greater stake
in the environment than children: it is their world which adults
currently threaten. On the other hand it is all too easy for children
to be placed in the position either of helpless victims or fodder
for adult-controlled campaigns. The two contributions which
follow tread this line carefully. One puts us in touch directly
with contemporary practice, the other puts children and environmental issues in the context of community action in Britain.

Katy Green's study of traffic calming in Leicester shows how it
is possible to ensure that the technical features of traffic calming
remain subservient to the goals and values of the project – to create
safer play areas for children. It is an inspiring example, not least
because it demonstrates that, given the political will and a high
level of co-operation between communities and agencies, it is
possible to make a tangible and relatively simple improvement
to children's lives.

Yet why do we not see more examples of this kind of project
up and down the country? The answer lies in the combination
of vested and personal interests which object to such projects or
which do not recognise their value. That is why there is an urgent
need for education and awareness raising on environmental
matters, and why communities have to get involved too.

It is the latter theme which informs Jim Radford's chapter.
Drawing on his own experience, he makes the case for children's
involvement in community action and community projects in
ways which do not depend on adult control. Children need information, support and encouragement to become involved in this
way. Indeed the chapter ends by showing the potential for
children's action on the environment to develop in a community
setting after it has been initiated within a school.

Both chapters point the way forward for a community development approach to children and the environment. They make
explicit the genuine, pivotal role of children, provided they are
given information and structures by adults. The chapters show
that children's involvement in environmental issues in community
settings can work. Above all, they remind us of the need to keep
environmental issues firmly on the political agenda, forcing

adults in general and politicians in particular to take the long-term view of society and the planet seriously.

References

Leach, P. (1994) *Children First*, London: Michael Joseph.

Roome, N. (1993) 'Green Perspectives on Community and Public Policy' in *Community and Public Policy*, eds. Butcher, H., Glen A., Henderson P., and Smith J., London: Pluto Press in association with CDF/BICC.

4 Children and Traffic Calming

Katy Green

The outdoor environment is children's traditional playspace, as we know from old pictures and films of cities as late as the 1970s. Yet in the 1990s – the decade of the environment – we have begun to persuade ourselves that it is wrong to see children playing outside. We keep children in, at who knows what cost to their development, rather than changing a situation we have created.

Children have to play. A game of tig, or let's pretend, does not just develop physical balance, strength and co-ordination, but also vital social, creative and intellectual skills. Through play children understand how to operate in a social group; they invent and memorise; they use rhythm, symbols, strategy, colour, materials and words. Once we have grown up we tend to forget that we had to learn to be everything that we are. The journey from babyhood to adult member of complex society is a very long one indeed.

Home (usually family) and formal education (usually school) are two other fundamental experiences for children, and both offer all kinds of formal and informal skills. Play is the way children apply and make sense of it all. Even as adults, we rarely get a new washing machine and read the instructions first. Almost everyone plays with a new thing to understand how it works, and intricate human physical and social behaviour requires years of exploration and practice.

Play begins at home. By the time children are at school (and what with weekends, evenings and holidays about three-quarters of childhood time is spent out of school) the outdoor environment is their preferred arena for play. This is why the neighbourhood forms of children's play discussed by Joe Hasler in Chapter 10 below is so important. Children like backyards, gardens and play areas, but naturally head for opportunities to cope with the real world – other people, new challenges, life at large. We put them at greater eventual risk if we try to remove all manageable risk. Children have to fall and argue and learn to recognise danger so they can survive as adults.

Necessary risk is not at all the same as unnecessary danger. Children want and need to play near home, outside, within reach of trusted adults, with access to other children and city life. Yet our residential streets are filled with cars, at a speed limit of 30 miles per hour, which can easily kill a child. Many city residential areas are now so unpleasant and empty of people that parents are frightened to let their children out. The streets look dangerous, even though fears of abduction are very much larger than actual occurrence.

Research published by the Policy Studies Institute (Hillman et al., 1990) has shown that children's mobility and independence have been drastically eroded in the last two decades. In 1971, 80 per cent of seven and eight year olds went to school without adult supervision. By 1990 this figure had fallen to 9 per cent. Adults have been steadily increasing the amount of time they spend driving their children, thereby increasing the very traffic dangers they fear. And as fewer children walk about the city unescorted, those that do are more vulnerable.

Anyone working with children, and anyone who can remember how they spent their own childhood, cannot fail to be aware of all this. There has been some debate on the issues, but Britain has lagged behind some of its European neighbours in tackling the situation. The little that has been done has tended to emphasise 'safety education', teaching children to cross the road and so on. On its own, this approach is limited. Children are not responsible for traffic, and can only go some way towards reducing its dangers.

Traffic Calming

In 1989, however, the Department of Transport agreed a target to reduce all traffic casualties by a third by the year 2000, and set about releasing some funds to local authorites for 'traffic-calming' measures, to slow down motor traffic.

We could still learn from the approach, if not the techniques, of other European countries with regard to traffic and people. In particular, the Dutch government has experimented over ten years with *woonerven*, which are residential areas created out of an existing street, where cars, vans, adults and children have equal priority. The Dutch have worked on small areas so that mistakes can be contained, and have evaluated what they do. There have been high legal standards for the improvements, and even government funded research on how and where children play. Of course not all the experiments have been an unqualified success but, importantly, work continues, with the country as whole learning from the mistakes.

Ways to 'calm' or slow down traffic now used in Britain include: speed ramps or humps in the road of varying lengths; chicanes which narrow the road on one or both sides; pavement extensions (or footway extensions, as engineers sometimes call them); signs; traffic islands, entrance treatments to slow traffic entering streets. Other design features like planters, different kinds of paving, pedestrianisation, bollards and so on can be included.

The DoT funding – which should continue to be available during the 1990s – has caused much debate within local authority departments on how and where traffic calming should be used. Increasingly, there are also attempts by the more enlightened to broaden the concept of traffic calming to include other environmental improvements, so that we follow (or even lead) the European example of outdoor living areas and 'green' cities. The even more enlightened are also aware that there is no real division between the social and the environmental, and are raising the issue of how, and how far, local residents should be consulted over work to improve the areas they live in. But children rarely feature in such discussions.

Children Today Projects

Meanwhile, in 1990 (quite by coincidence) three Children Today Projects were set up by the National Children's Play and Recreation Unit, which is a short-term almost-quango hosted by the Sports Council as a government concesssion to children's play. Children Today Projects were based in Devon, the North West and Leicestershire. Each was given three staff, two years and the somewhat broad brief to improve things to do with children's play. Each ran a number of projects focusing on different aspects. In Leicester the Street Play project aimed to connect the widespread concern for children's place in the environment with the newly established DoT target, and the debate around traffic calming techniques.

In order to do some 'real' work with 'real' children, the Street Play Project planned to make three city streets more safe and interesting for children's play. The project would consult both adults and children living in the streets, and ensure that the work could act as pilot for future traffic calming work.

Indeed, the Street Play Project was kept in full view of the local authority throughout its existence, and much of the project's first year was spent not only raising funds but also trying to convince City Council officers and other bodies of its relevance. The issues of children and streets, play and traffic calming are cross-departmental; engineering, planning, leisure and housing departments all have influence on and responsibility to the streets and those who live in them. It has to be said that leisure services departments in particular – usually the departments who hold much of the expertise on children's play needs and community issues – are generally absent from the debates on environmental improvements and traffic calming issues.

Once persuaded of the relevance of the work to their jobs, City Council officers were usually helpful with time and resources. The planning work was streamlined as much as possible (for a pilot) so that their support – and residents' – was not abused.

While, in the spirit of play, it was important to allow mistakes to be made, unnecessary mistakes had to be avoided, since it was people's own streets that were to be messed about with. A great deal of thought went into selecting the streets to be worked on. Every household (and local business) in the three streets was informed of the project and asked for objections. Only one objection was received, from among 300 households. Two public meetings were held for local residents to explain the issues involved.

Through this process a small number of residents, including some children, came forward to work with Children Today over the next six months to decide, plan and prepare the consultation process. Residents not involved in planning were kept informed of progress through two newsletters, distributed to every household.

The most useful resource for working with both officers and residents was a book of photographs by Shirley Baker (1989) called *Street Photographs, Manchester and Salford*. The photographs were all taken in terraced streets during the 1960s and 1970s and show children of all ages at a huge variety of play at all times of the day and year. The most hardened of adults responded to the photographs, sometimes with reminiscences of their own childhood play.

Consultation was the core of the project. The knowledge of people who live in an area is invaluable, and it is unlikely that real and lasting improvements can be made without linking that close knowledge with the technical expertise of planners and engineers. It was particularly important to draw attention to the fact that children's views can and should be sought. They, like women and the elderly, are most likely to use the environment close to the home, but hardly ever attend consultation meetings.

Adults also needed to be attracted, since they have more power than children to help or hinder change. Above all, the consultation had to be interesting and enjoyable to do – residents may perversely feel that they have better things to do, and local authorities are also under heavy time and financial pressures. The traffic calming money released by the DoT itself has to be spent within a matter of months by the time it actually gets into local authority hands. The focus of the project was to try to make the actual contact with residents 'quality' time so that neither City Council nor residents' time was wasted, yet useful information could be exchanged.

Efforts were also made to keep the cost realistically low, to prove that reasonable local consultation could take place every time improvements are made.

Consultation took place over May, June and July 1992. Altogether actual time with residents, including children, totalled only several hours but representative numbers of residents from all age groups and cultures gave their views. It was a four-stage process:

1. Outdoor Exhibition

Soft Touch Community Arts were commissioned to build a reusable weatherproof exhibition with panels at child (and wheelchair user) height as well as full height. It contained pictures of street designs, ramps, paving, trees, ideas for the play area, to give people some idea of what 'traffic calming' means and what changes are possible. It was held outside the school and in the streets, attended by City Council officers who were there to answer questions. It attracted large numbers of adults and children, over much shorter periods than similar exhibitions housed in indoor venues.

2. *Priority Search Survey*

All households should have the opportunity to give ideas, even if they choose not to, and a survey can encourage people to contribute in their own homes. A number of different surveys were considered, but most asked people for problems instead of solutions. The Priority Search Survey was chosen because it was made up of residents' own ideas. Two sessions were held in the school to gather children's ideas, and adults – who did not turn up for more formal meetings – gave their ideas when approached outside the school and in the streets.

The resulting 38-statement questionnaire was taken to every household. SAEs and personal collection ensured between 40 and 50 per cent return over a few days. A number of residents distributed the surveys themselves to neighbours. Interpreters (Medway Community Mobile staff and Home/School Liaison Officers) took the questionnaire to Asian households whose first language was not English. This was time consuming – an interpreted questionnaire took up to an hour to complete – but it also enabled a closer link to be built up with residents. Analysis of results gave us overall priorities as well as what different ages, genders or ethnic groups felt were priorities.

Children liked the survey immensely. They were pleased to recognise some of their own ideas, and seemed simply to enjoy the process of comparing one idea against another. They were also markedly helpful to each other, working together on questions that some found difficult. We completed the survey with them by going into their school and spending two one-hour sessions with them.

Adults, on the other hand, frequently got bored by the length of the survey. Priority Search is based on the theory that a preference can be identified most effectively by repeating it three times against different possibilities. The front sheet of the survey gave a brief explanation of this, but people remained unconvinced that it was not the result of pure stupidity.

Another disadvantage was the difficulty of giving the statements equal 'weight'; several residents said they found it difficult to decide between statements such as 'sand and water on the play area' and 'stop bullying'. And if 'stop bullying' appears as an option, people will tick it because they do not agree with bullying. This may not necessarily mean that they or their children are experiencing bullying.

3. Models

The fact that survey statements came from residents themselves is in itself a limitation, in the same way that suggestions from non-local engineers are limited. There is no reason why, after all, residents should be up on the latest in traffic-calming techniques.

We wanted to use models so that both children and adults could visualise possibilities and develop ideas from the initial reactions contained in the questionnaire. They particularly needed to talk to the recently set-up design team made up of City Council engineers, planners, a landscape architect, a play area designer and a housing officer.

We based the idea on some of the work done by 'Planning for Real' but recognised that models should be robust enough for children to play with, and that the issues discussed are neither clear cut nor easy. In this project it was not the case that residents, even children, would necessarily be 'right' nor council officers 'wrong'. Our hopeful aim was some kind of mutual cataclysm, a connection of residents with officers, which together might produce solutions that could never have been born if one or the other had worked alone.

Soft Touch Community Arts were again commissioned, this time to make 1:72 scale models of the three streets and the play area. They used cheap wood so that the basic framework could be used again. It was personalised by pasting photographs of the actual houses on to the fronts. Once the perspective had been worked out this was quite simple to do and both children and adults really liked the result.

We held four sessions with the models. Two two-hour sessions with 8 to 11 year olds were structured via the school, followed by two more 'public' sessions for both children and adults. As usual, hardly anyone attended the indoor session we held, but when we took the models out on a sunny Saturday on the local play area people came in much larger numbers and there was much debate.

We supplied a collection of modelling materials, but only the children tended actually to make things they wanted to see. Adults used the models as a focus for discussion. There were people at each session who were used to working with children, and they were able to translate the thinking behind even the wildest and most impractical ideas, which often revealed a logical under-standing of the problems. Other ideas the children came up with for both streets and play area were immediately practical. They became used to the vocabulary of traffic calming very quickly, and conversed knowledgeably about chicanes and ramps.

Children's play range extends quickly as they grow, from very close to the home at a pre-school age, to a radius of about 400 yards by the time they are eight or nine, and much further as they reach adolescence. The younger children tended to concentrate on the areas close to where they lived, and older children worked on the whole street. It is possible – but at the time was not monitored – that the small scale of the model enabled children and adults to see themselves as part of a wider area.

We concluded that a less detailed model would have served the same purposes. The photographs alone were enough to make the street 'realistic' and encourage people to say what they thought. We originally included even model wheely bins because we hoped people would come up with solutions to their storage that have so far eluded planners and engineers. But wheely bins – or rather, disposal of rubbish in crowded inner-city areas – seem to be insoluble problems

The most successful part of the models was the debate they enabled and the sense of 'event' they created, as well as the number of ideas that we gathered from them. Residents argued over the issues with each other and with the officers, but the argument never became aggressive. Facilitators were necessary, however, to encourage and translate ideas, and to ensure that both adults and children worked on both the streets and the play area – there was a slight tendency for adults to see their streets as theirs, and the play area as the children's. We kept written and photo-graphic records of all the comments people came up with.

Originally we had wanted to consult all age groups in the street. In the end, we had to target to some extent, though we excluded no one. Working through Medway Junior School we consulted most 8 to 11-year-olds in the street, although we also obtained the views of some younger and older children. Adults, via the survey or the models, tended to self-select, and by far the greatest interest came from the 26 to 39 age group.

Because the events were mainly held outside it was almost impossible for any resident to be unaware that the consultation was taking place, even if they chose not to attend. This put some responsibility on the residents as well as the officers, so that the process was not tied up by accusations or fears of being unrepre-sentative or elitist.

Of course, inequality does exist and some extra effort has to be made by those consulting. We were careful to publicise each event with easily understood publicity, to build up a trusted relationship with the children through the school, to ensure a welcoming atmosphere, to have staff able to translate or work well with children, and to maintain an approachable and easily recognised presence throughout the project. The Home/School Liaison Officers and Medway Community Mobile staff were invaluable in helping involve the Bengali, Gujerati and Punjabi speaking residents. Of course, a strong community with confident residents will always be easier to consult. Consultation cannot take the place of good long-term community work.

4. The Brief

Perhaps the hardest part of all was to pull together all the many and sometimes contradictory comments into an intelligible brief. Most of the design team had been present at most of the consultation events. After cutting out the very wildest and unaffordable ideas, they helped to form a realistic brief. Issues beyond the scope of the project, such as bullying, supervised play and street cleanliness were passed on to relevant departments.

Funding was too low to make big changes; and a compromise had to be reached between the children who in the main wanted no traffic at all and the adults who rarely wanted radical change, to the streets at least.

The plans include ramps at either end of the street, and a 12 metre 'speed table' or elongated ramp in the middle of each street, extending the pavements to allow only one lane of traffic at those points. The extended pavements incorporate interesting coloured paving designs, decorative bars, trees, and small, cemented-in boulders. If funding allows, a decorative archway or sign will warn drivers they are entering a residential area where children are playing. The design tries to slow traffic, use items of play value and extend the amount of space for children while enabling adult residents to use and park cars. The play area – still an absolute necessity in crowded city streets – offers further opportunities for exploration and more adventurous games. The outdoor exhibition was put to use again to show residents the draft plans and to note their comments.

The street designs are ones that could easily be incorporated in future traffic-calming spending, though it remains to be seen how well they encourage children's play, and how popular they

are with different ages of residents. Evaluation is important in conjunction with repeated local consultation as each area is traffic
calmed, so that future traffic-calming money can really benefit
the quarter of Leicester's citizens who are children.

A great deal of the project's time was taken up raising funds.
The traffic-calming money available from the Department of
Transport is being targeted at high accident areas; the three streets
we worked on did not have a high enough accident rate. Urban
Programme supplied the bulk of the funding, and the remainder
came from Leicester City Council.

It is difficult to give a conclusive cost as the project was a pilot.
The total cost for consultation, design and construction for three
streets and one play area (excluding most, but not all, staff costs)
was about £90,000. Normal work to use traffic-calming funds will
not include a play area. Staffing for events was usually supplied
by Leicester City Council, within usual duties.

Conclusion

In some ways the project raised as many questions about consultation as it answered. What is consultation? It is never neutral
– no local authority goes out with a blank mind to a homogenous
group of residents who all agree on the issues.

The aim of the Street Play Project was to value residents'
knowledge at least as highly as that of officers, but it was a campaigning project with a clear aim to improve streets for children,
and to value children's ideas particularly. There were residents who
did not want the streets improved. There were residents – of
course – who thought and continue to think that children should
not be allowed to play in the streets. Several residents did not want
trees because they have leaves and berries and attract birds –
arguments to floor many an environmentalist.

There are often reasons in the apparently unreasonable: some
women still clean the pavement outside their houses, and see
themselves responsible for cleaning up dog and bird droppings.
Someone who has worked for a car which represents power and
mobility does not want children fiddling with it. If the only
patch of the world people can control is in and around their house,
they will argue for their right to park precisely outside their own
front door. It is not unusual in our country to see children and

their welfare as the responsibility only of their parents, rather than as the nation's future, good or bad. Nevertheless most of these views are shortsighted; should they hold as much sway as the longer, braver view?

There were a few residents, children among them, who had ideas which extended the boundaries of traffic calming, and whose practical imagination and vision went far beyond that of their neighbours. It has to be admitted they were in a minority. Is the majority always right?

In other ways the project was a public relations tool, and I argued its efficacy as such. At the big outdoor model session children and adults played spot-the-council-officer: they look like normal people! In order to do their jobs well it is important that council officers grow used to communicating constantly with the residents of the city they serve, so they work together rather than against each other. But it would be naive not to recognise that the council is run by political parties with their own agendas. Individually and collectively, many officers have more power and information than many residents, and can abuse them and ignore their needs – though many do not.

Officers conceded that they are often able to ignore objections raised. If consultation is a paper exercise, people learn to distrust it, and spend any contact time with officers attacking the council. On the other hand, it is not helpful to attack council officers before they have even opened their mouths, which happens at some consultation meetings.

We did not aim for consensus. There can be deep-rooted conflicts within communities, not least between children and adults, which can only be tackled on a long-term basis.

I think that what our 'consultation' achieved was to begin to increase information exchange and debate in order to get better designed improvements that could benefit children. Outdoor exhibitions, models and surveys proved to be three reasonably cost-effective and enjoyable ways of doing so.

But the work is there to be improved upon. There have been worrying suggestions that consultation of children has now been 'done'. This is not the case. Every area is different. The enormous specialist expertise held within different council departments reaches its potential only if consistently used in conjunction with residents of all ages, towards the same end of making a city worth living in.

References

Baker, S. (1989) *Street Photographs, Manchester and Salford,* Newcastle: Bloodaxe Books.

Hillman, M., Adams, J. and Whiteleg, J. (1990) *One False Move . . . A Study of Children's Independent Mobility,* London: Policy Studies Institute.

5 Children and the Environment

Jim Radford

Unwelcome developments, which are likely to have an adverse effect on many people's lives, seem to gain our interest and to burgeon rapidly. Events like war, recession and the discovery of the AIDS virus, and decisions like the pit closure and privatisation programmes, have quickly been followed by public awareness leading to debate. This has focused attention on the possible effects and sometimes influenced them. Developments which serve to improve people's lives, on the other hand, are often part of a long slow process of change and may pass virtually unnoticed by those who are not directly involved.

In a similar way, there can be an enormous difference between the passing of a piece of legislation or the declaration of an international agreement and its implementation in ways which are meaningful to ordinary people. The latter can take a very long time, and require the mobilisation of a great deal of pressure and education.

The UN Convention on the Rights of the Child and the UK government's commitment at the 1992 Earth Summit to implement Agenda 21 are cases in point. Agenda 21 is about the adoption of 'national sustainability strategies' and includes increasing the participation of children and young people in matters of environmental policy. Both the Convention and Agenda 21 are of major importance. The Convention recognises the basic right of children to food, clean water, health care, education and an adequate standard of living, in an environment that allows them to develop. It is clearly based upon the concept of children as participating members of society and not as merely the passive recipients of treatment. For anyone familiar with the harsh reality of deprived children on the neglected inner-city estates, or in the bed and breakfast hotels and cold shop doorways of post-Thatcher Britain, the Convention makes wonderful reading. It seems almost too good to be true, and of course it is!

It is this issue of the gap between expressed intentions and realities on the ground that I want to address in my discussion of children and the environment. Another way of seeing it is as an exploration of the connections, or lack of them, between social policies and local communities.

In Britain we make a fairly rigid distinction between parliamentary and extra-parliamentary politics. Those who engage in national and international campaigns for legislative changes are involved in a necessary activity. To achieve results they must focus on specific objectives and, like many specialists, may come to believe that theirs is the only contribution that matters. When the final vote is taken and the agreement or law that they have worked for has been passed, it is understandable that our elected representatives should relax and congratulate themselves on the successful completion of their campaign, before transferring their attention to the next issue on their agenda.

Yet often the real campaign is just beginning. Women did not become equal when they were given the vote. Discrimination against black people did not cease when the Race Relations Act became law. Between the fine words and good intentions of legislatures and their application for the benefit of individuals there stands an army of administrators, lawyers and budget holders with narrow purse strings, all ready to explain: why Acts do not mean what they seem to say; why this clause does not apply in one case and that clause is superseded in another; and how words like 'proper', 'adequate', 'appropriate', 'eligible' or 'suitable' can mean exactly what some bureaucrat or minister wants them to mean.

A fairly safe guide is that any legislation which reduces the rights, benefits or freedoms of ordinary people will stand a very good chance of being enforced without community pressure, while those that increase rights and entitlements are much more likely to be delayed or ignored without it.

The Position of Children

Every ordinary citizen is at a disadvantage in his or her dealings with corporate power, whether it be the state, local government or big business. Children suffer additional disadvantages. First, they do not have the same rights as adults, or are not regarded as having those rights, which amounts to the same thing. Secondly, outside the education system, the organs of the state do not regard it as their duty to keep children informed about matters which affect them, or to consult them, even when they are affected more than adults. Thirdly, although children are constantly organised by adults, at home, in school or in the local youth club, they rarely have access to the kind of organisational help and collective power that adults can call upon. In general, children are discouraged from participating in many aspects of community life and especially in those areas that some of their elders see as controversial.

There are many reasons for this, not least the tradition which says that children should be seen and not heard, which persists in the view that they should be told rather than consulted. That situation will not change because the UN Convention on the Rights of the Child has been ratified by the British government and has therefore been accepted as official policy. After all it is the government's policy to revitalise the economy, to provide training places for every jobless teenager, to improve the health service, to house the homeless, to reduce crime, and so forth. Significant change will take place only if the rights contained in the Convention are made widely known and if there is community pressure for them to be put into effect.

The creation of the Children's Rights Development Unit (CRDU) to promote both implementation and awareness of the Convention was a valuable step in that direction. However, we should beware of placing too much reliance on high-level pressure groups. Many of them, and CRDU is a good example, are very professional but, like politicians, they find it necessary to focus their efforts and to choose their targets. More often than not the targets chosen are government departments and agencies with responsibility for providing services. The representations and consultation documents may be well researched and thorough, but faced with a long list of recommendations which all seem to call for the allocation of extra resources even the most sympathetic chief officer is inclined to come up with good reasons why they are unnecessary, impractical or impossible!

Many readers will be familiar with the government recycling process in which existing provision that has been shown to be inadequate is simply repackaged and relaunched, with the same or less money, in order to describe it as something new and better. In the last resort, as we now see regularly in the health service and local government, officials are increasingly ready to throw up their hands and say bluntly 'we just cannot afford it'.

This is not to suggest that comprehensive representation at high levels will not have beneficial effects, but it will have much more effect if it is supported and complemented by widespread local, individual and group pressure. The experience of many campaigns shows that this can lead to a piecemeal pattern of improvements, concessions and reform, which the government sooner or later will have to incorporate into its wider policies and programmes. This will happen only if there is a significant increase in awareness and expectations.

Of all the issues that affect children and in which they might wish to participate the environment is arguably the most obvious. Indeed, on many environmental issues they could reasonably claim a greater right to be heard and involved than adults. Not only do children suffer more from the deterioration that is taking place in the local environment, to which they are more closely confined, but on the national and global scale it is they who will have to deal with the consequences of the inadequate short-term policies that are currently being pursued by their elders. Furthermore, evidence is accumulating to show that concern about the environment is high on the agenda of children. The consultation document produced by the Children's Rights Development Unit (1993) notes that 'there is considerable interest in local neighbourhood issues, especially conservation and safety, and there is much distress caused by the apparent lack of long term policies to protect the wider environment'. These are crucially important points. In 1993 the Department of the Environment launched a new initiative to encourage children to take environmental action, and a summit and a competition were organised. However, unless this kind of programme is accompanied by long-term support for work with children in local communities its impact will be ephemeral.

In his book *Children and the Environment* Martin Rosenbaum (1993) has identified and examined the environmental dangers which threaten children in the UK and particularly those caused by the massive volume of pollutants that are continuously being released into the air, land, and sea. The list is horrendous: lead, nitrates, bacteria, nitrogen oxide, sulphur dioxide, carbon monoxide, benzene, dioxins, ozone, asbestos, radiation and more. He quotes authorities from UNICEF to the BMA to show that children are far more vulnerable to toxic pollution than adults, and quotes statistics to show that the arbitrary official 'safety levels', which many experts regard as inadequate, are commonly exceeded.

Children are not only exposed to pollution more than adults, but they suffer adverse effects at much lower levels of exposure and their bodies are far less efficient at neutralising and eliminating the toxins they ingest. The evidence that Rosenbaum has chronicled shows that mounting pollution is seriously affecting the health, intelligence and mortality of British children. If we add to the deadly cocktail of invisible poisons the toll of deaths, injuries, bronchial disease and life restricting congestion that is caused by the remorseless growth in traffic, and throw in the known effects of inadequate housing and poverty, it is clear that for many children the environment has become an unsafe and unfriendly place in which to grow up. If it had occurred to anyone to consult children about this 'development', it seems unlikely that many would have given it their approval. It is not surprising that campaigning environmental organisations draw attention to the vulnerability of children to radiation-linked diseases such as leukaemia, foetal malformation and other genetic defects. In its response to the decision to license the Thorp nuclear reprocessing plant at Sellafield, Greenpeace commented that, because of their vulnerability, children protect adults, 'acting as some awful human early warning device'.

Children's Involvement

The argument against consulting or involving children is usually that they do not have the information, understanding or maturity to make balanced judgements. Leaving aside the fact that this applies to many adults, children are often more aware of the local environment and its shortcomings than their parents, if only because they spend more time in it. If they are unaware of and uninvolved in options and efforts to change it, this may be because no one has bothered to inform and recruit them.

In some cultures it is quite normal for 13- or 14-year-olds to take on adult responsibilities. Few British parents would want to burden children so young, but in their mixed desire to protect and control children, adults are often guilty of denying children's readiness to learn and to contribute. Most children know that they have much to learn. They learn faster if their interest is aroused and if they are encouraged to participate and put their knowledge to use.

Every child has first-hand knowledge of his or her immediate environment. They become aware of its limitations and physical hazards at an early age. Their parents teach them that to step off the pavement could mean death or injury. They soon discover for themselves that streets and vehicles are dirty and dangerous, and that opportunities for carefree play are limited. If they live in overcrowded or damp accommodation on a run-down estate, or in an area with few community facilities and crumbling schools, they suffer the many disadvantages this entails. Apart from the early stages of this learning process, in which parents are crucially involved, children usually have to teach themselves the art of urban survival. In most cases there is little encouragement for them to engage in remedial action.

Children learn about the wider environment at second hand but here the situation is reversed. They receive information and encouragement from many sources and especially at school, where their curiosity about animals and nature is used to interest and involve them in global conservation issues. Television programmes about the environment add to their knowledge and arouse their concern because they can connect these with what they are being taught in history, geography, science and nature studies, as well as in conservation projects.

By their early teens most intelligent youngsters are aware of the importance of clean air and water, and that neither can be taken for granted. They know about the dangers of radiation, the effects of acid rain and the urgent need to preserve the rain forests and the ozone layer. They are often better informed than their parents about the ecological chain of cause and effect, and they worry about the disappearing habitats that threaten the existence of many species.

It is the general view of the establishment that children should not be involved in politically contentious matters and, since community campaigns are invariably seen as politically con-tentious by those whose policies are being challenged, this view is used to exclude them from all but anodyne attempts to improve their own environment. The hypocrisy of this position is exposed by the positive encouragement given by the same quarter when children are involved in global conservation issues. Teachers and youth workers who recruit children to 'Save the Whale', or to oppose mining and logging in the Amazon, can look for a commendation from the Duke of Edinburgh, in spite of the fact that these campaigns are politically contentious in Norway and Brazil! If the same workers were to involve children in local housing action campaigns or in demands for improved services, they could expect condemnation and reprimands.

However, it is not establishment disapproval that prevents children from participating in community action so much as the failure of adult organisers and local groups to stimulate their involvement by informing and consulting them. This does happen when the objectives are specifically to help children, as in attempts to create adventure playgrounds or to prevent school mergers and closures, but children are more often left out of broader campaigns and rarely encouraged to organise themselves, as they did successfully in the school strikes during the First World War.

Where children have been significantly involved in a community initiative from the beginning, as in many of the local road safety campaigns, they seem to have adapted quickly and enthusiastically to the process of collective action. Young teenagers, in particular, are often very capable and much more perceptive than many adults expect them to be. Reading Craig Russell's description in Chapter 8 below of children's involvement in the march through Moss Side and Hulme after the funeral of the murdered 14 year old, Benji Stanley, underlines this point.

I write with hindsight. Like many community workers I have often been guilty of planning campaigns and recruiting adult participants to deal with issues that were equally or more important to children. I did so not because I was unaware of this fact, but because I thought adults would be more disciplined and motivated, and that their representation would carry more weight. My experience over the years has caused me to revise that view. It is obviously the case that a group of unruly youngsters can disrupt a meeting and be difficult to control, but so can a group of undisciplined tenants. Everyone needs to be inducted to the democratic process – why not sooner than later? It is also true that young people often need more basic information and encouragement to become motivated, but when they do their commitment and application can surpass that of adults. In some cases action and representation by children has proved to be more effective than that by adults, if only because it was patently sincere and less easy to dismiss as politically inspired.

King Hill Campaign

My first experience of the initiative and determination that
children can show in a common cause was back in 1965, at the
height of the seminal direct action campaign which brought an
end to the general practice of separating and destroying homeless
families. This was being done by the simple process of excluding
husbands and older sons from homeless accommodation and
automatically evicting wives and mothers after three months, when
the younger children would be taken into care.

The campaign centred on King Hill hostel, a dilapidated ex-army
camp in remote Kent, which served the whole county as homeless
accommodation. In 1965 it contained 75 desperate women and
more than 200 children in squalid conditions, all waiting their
turn to be evicted. In protest at this inhumane treatment and after
representation had failed, an action group was formed which
helped the excluded husbands to rejoin their wives and children,
by moving them into the hostel in defiance of its rules. The
united families were organised to resist all attempts to evict them,
and to occupy the hostel until its workhouse rules and procedures
were scrapped. The campaign attracted national and international attention and after a year-long struggle, in which several
men were sent to prison for defying injunctions to abandon their
families, it succeeded in all its objectives.

Throughout the occupation children of all ages attended the
frequent meetings. Most decisions were taken by their parents,
but the children voluntarily took on the task of erecting barricades
and of blocking the path of police and county council officers
whenever they tried to enter the hostel to make arrests or to evict
families. Faced with an impenetrable mass of shouting children
jammed into the corridor between them and their objective, the
officials invariably retreated. In spite of the seriousness of the
situation it seemed that many of the children regarded it as a great
game and I did not argue with critics who accused us of using them.
I too thought we were using them, albeit in the children's own
best interests.

This attitude changed suddenly when one of the children was
knocked down and killed outside the hostel gates on her way to
school. One of the ancillary complaints in the charter of demands
that we had presented to the council months earlier was that
children were being forced to walk over a mile to the village
school, along an unpaved and dangerous road. Their parents had

called for a zebra crossing, street lights and a 30 mph speed limit, to no avail.

When I heard of the tragedy I went straight to the hostel. The adults had called an emergency meeting – but the children had already acted. After months of listening to discussions about direct action tactics, they had known exactly what to do without any prompting. Outside the hostel gates they had painted their own zebra crossing and warning signs, while the no limit signs for half a mile in either direction had been overpainted with a bold 30. When the council sent a tar sprayer to obliterate the crossing, it was repainted within hours. I don't know how many children took part in this operation, but it was obviously a team effort and one that eventually produced the desired result, when the council caved in on the speed limit and installed proper warning signs. Thereafter I saw the children as important participants in the campaign.

Children's Capacity

I have helped to involve children in a number of community initiatives since then, but I am not a youth worker and this has rarely been a priority for the group. It has usually been in the context of predominantly adult activity in which they took most of the decisions and the children were willing spear carriers and demonstrators. Their contribution was valued but in retrospect I believe I could have done more to develop it.

As the press officer for various campaigns, including the Family Squatting Movement, and at staged events like the occupation of Centre Point in central London, I have noted and used the fact that the involvement of children creates valuable photo opportunities and that it helps to achieve more, and sympathetic, press coverage for the issue. I have also observed that their presence at presentations and in lobbying can help to produce a more reasonable response from councillors and officers. On the other hand it sometimes elicits a patronising response which older children are quick to recognise and criticise.

In recent years I have witnessed children's ability to organise and represent themselves, but this first came about only by accident. In 1990 I organised a survey on a council estate in Ealing, West London, where I hoped to revive a moribund tenants' association. The most common complaint was about the activities of a particular group of youngsters who roamed the streets together. The crimes attributed to them ranged from burglary, noise and harassment, to throwing bricks at the tenants' hall.

With the help of Mary Hogan, a local community worker who lived on the estate, we brought the children together to hear their side of the story. They turned out to be perfectly normal boys and girls, mostly 12- to 13-years-old, led by one or two boisterous spirits who attracted attention and sometimes got into trouble because they had nothing to do and nowhere to go. They hung around outside the tenants' hall because it was one of the few open spaces and they were not allowed inside. They had their own ideas about what the estate needed. Above all, they told us, they wanted a place where they could meet and talk and do things, where they could organise their own discos, and be out of the public eye.

This seemed reasonable, and since the tenants' hall was under-used it seemed obvious that an approach should be made to the tenants' management committee to see if the children could use it on certain evenings. The youngsters readily accepted advice that it would be necessary to convince the tenants that they were properly organised and that they would use the building responsibly. They elected a committee, appointed officers from among themselves and named their newly formed organisation 'South Ealing Youth Action'.

There was some prejudice against the group among the elderly tenants on the management committee, and in most circumstances I would have volunteered to negotiate with them on the children's behalf. In this case that was not a good idea. I had recently incurred the hostility of the local Conservative councillor by chairing a public meeting on the Housing Act which he had not enjoyed. I knew that he would be influential at the management committee meeting and that he would oppose anything I recommended. Mary Hogan felt that she was similarly suspect.

At her suggestion, but with serious misgivings on my part, we put it to the youngsters that it might be better if they presented their own case to the tenants. None of them had ever done anything like that before but they immediately decided that they would, and set about preparing for it with meticulous attention to detail. Three spokespersons were carefully chosen and rehearsed, and tactics were discussed at length.

When the presentation finally took place I was able to observe from the back of the hall. My fingers were crossed but I need not have worried. The young people knew exactly what they wanted and what assurances the tenants needed to hear. They made their case directly and honestly, and they answered the questions that were put to them convincingly. They got the use of the hall. We had both learnt a valuable lesson.

I was so influenced by this experience that when I met a group of older teenagers with the same need shortly afterwards, I told them about it. This encouraged them to create their own organisation, 'Hanwell Youth Action', and to make a similar presentation to the Hanwell Community Centre, which was equally successful. My colleague, the local community worker, has since achieved exactly the same result with another group in Northolt.

Although I have always believed that young people have as much right to participate in community affairs as anyone else, my appreciation of their potential ability to do so effectively, and to organise and speak for themselves when necessary, came rather late in the day. It has prompted me to consider why children are not more involved in improving the environment that affects them most: the community they live in.

Many are involved, of course, usually in projects controlled by adults, but sometimes in autonomous youth groups such as those I have described and occasionally as individuals. The *Guardian* (21 October 1993), for example, carried a report about two brothers, Alex and Andrew Caldecott, aged 11 and 15, who were sueing the waste disposal company Rechem International for contaminating their home in Pontypool with emissions of PCBs and dioxins, which damage the quality of their life and increase their risk of future cancer. They obviously have the support of their parents but nevertheless have become principal actors in an action that could affect everyone who lives near industrial plants.

If some children can take effective action so could many more, but they need information, support and encouragement to do it. The voluntary sector is best able to supply this and to motivate children, not by treating them as adults but by regarding them as equally important participants in community action and by taking positive steps to promote and welcome their involvement. Community workers are usually well placed to provide organisational help, and youth workers are even better placed to stimulate interest and to foster initiatives. In my view, far too many of the latter have settled for the soft option of catering for safe recreational interests while steering children away from anything controversial.

One could make the same criticism of teachers, who are obviously in a better position than anyone to influence children's interests, but I do not think it would be justified. Many of today's teachers are strongly committed to participatory methods. They are keen to involve their pupils in meaningful activity that will improve the environment and local conditions, as well as creating wider opportunities for learning and self-expression. In many areas, teachers are working hard to involve parents and children in the achievement of common purposes, and to establish the school as an integral part of the local community. If their efforts are confined mainly to officially approved objectives, it is because of the constraints imposed upon teachers by the priorities of their jobs, the demands of the curriculum and the watchful supervision of the educational bureaucracy; all these are much greater than those experienced by most community and youth workers.

In spite of this close monitoring, which obliges teachers to step warily around any issue which others hold to be contentious, the fact that some kinds of action to improve the environment are universally approved by all levels of the establishment has enabled many schools to involve their pupils in valuable projects.

School–Community Project

The Ripples scheme in Wandsworth is a good example of how teachers, children and parents can come together with community and environmental groups to identify local needs and to plan and implement their own solutions. The active participation of children is central to this scheme which has already transformed the environment around two schools. Like many community schemes it owes a great deal to the catalytic involvement of one individual, in this case a parent.

St Joseph's primary was a typically drab urban school with depressing surroundings. In 1992 its head set out to consult parents and children about the rebuilding programme and what might be done to improve the school environment. Steve Parry was one of the parents who responded with ideas and enthusiasm and who then volunteered his services and skills – to continue the process of consultation and to make things happen. Given that teachers have far too much on their plates to take on the demanding work of developing a major community development scheme, this was just the kind of luck that St Joseph's needed.

For the next year Steve worked without payment, involving and informing children, parents and local groups. He raised funds and created links with 150 organisations, drawing in suggestions and expertise from architects and planners, and enlisting the support of specialised bodies such as the Black Environment Network, staff and students at Kew Gardens, Learning through Landscapes and others.

Out of this intense activity has come a new school that is radically different from the old one, surrounded not by a dreary tarmac playground but by an outdoor classroom. The St Joseph's school garden has play areas, woodland paths, a pond, pergolas, an amphitheatre, a scale model of the solar system, colourful scented plants, recycling facilities and sheltered seats where children can sit and read. The heart of the new school is lit by a water-powered turbine – the first of its kind in Britain – that has been built at the delta of the river Wandle. This would have been impressive if imposed. The fact that it is the result of the combined efforts of children, teachers, parents and community groups means that it is doubly valued and that it has become the stimulus for further community development.

This is happening. The interest and support that was generated by the St Joseph's project led to the formal creation of Ripples, an independent voluntary organisation with a borough-wide brief 'to enable primary schools to develop initiatives and practical environmental projects, based upon the ideas, vision, needs and demands of their local communities'. A similar consultation process has produced equally detailed plans for West Hill School where the children were enthused by an organised visit to the Kew Gardens nature reserve in Sussex. Both of these projects should be fully implemented by the end of 1995, and a rolling programme of work with up to 70 schools is being planned for the next three years.

There are many lessons to be learned from the Ripples initiative. The fact that the St Joseph's and West Hill projects were not opposed by any political or vested interests did not reduce the need for the hard work and commitment that was necessary to create and maintain the high level of participation, but it obviously helped them to succeed. Sensible campaigners do not go out looking for opposition and it is often advisable to develop involvement and strength by focusing on practical achievable objectives that will attract the maximum support.

My views on community development strategy have always included the concept of building 'platforms' of achievement, confidence and organisational support from which the people involved can see further and may focus on larger tasks or wider issues. The success of Ripples represents such a platform and just as Steve Parry and his many associates have now raised their sights to look at the needs of schools and local communities throughout the borough, I am sure that the many children they have involved in decision making will be that much more likely, as they grow older, to claim and exercise their right to participate in other issues that concern them.

Children's Advice Centres?

Children who want to take initiatives will usually need help, advice and support from adults. In Wandsworth and in other areas that help is available but in many places it is not, or if it is the children do not know where to find it. It seems clear that schools and voluntary agencies could liaise and co-operate much more closely than most of them do, and this is an objective that youth workers, children's agencies and councils for voluntary service could usefully take on board.

One way of promoting it would be for either the local authority or a consortium of interested groups to set up a children's advice centre, perhaps within a Citizen's Advice Bureau or some other advice or development agency. Ideally this would be run by someone who could take on the role of a local children's ombudsman and who would be able to give children support and advice on how to go about changing and improving things. It could be initiated without additional resources by using an existing office and a suitable existing worker during specified hours.

The information that children might need would not be difficult to compile and is already filed in many agencies. The point of the experiment would be to provide the centre in a place that children would be likely to visit. If its existence and purpose were to be published in every school and at every youth venue I believe children would visit it. A local children's centre, if well promoted, could quickly become a focal point for teachers and parents as well as for children who wanted to get involved. By that stage it should not be too difficult to attract separate funding.

Children's concern for the environment can be a powerful motivating force. If we want the next generation to grow up in the confident belief that their views and actions can make a difference, we must learn from the Jesuits and help children to discover this at an early stage.

The case for a national childrens ombudsman has been made elsewhere (Gulbenkian, 1991). Local authorities could do their community and its children a great service by providing a local children's ombudsman, with a brief to support childrens' initiatives as well as their rights, and to advise them on how to go about changing and improving their local environment and where to get specialised help and resources. That would be a practical way of turning high-level policy declarations, such as the UN Convention on the Rights of the Child, into a reality at community level, a reality moreover which should be developed and shaped by children themselves.

References

Children's Rights Development Unit (1993) '*The Rights of Children and Young People to a Safe, Healthy Environment*', consultation document, London: CRDU, p. 6.

C. Gulbenkian Foundation (1991) *Taking Children Seriously*, London: Gulbenkian Foundation.

Rosenbaum, M. (1993) *Children and the Environment*, London: National Children's Bureau.

Historically, education can lay claim to being the professional sector with the strongest roots in the community. Community schools, community service – community education in general – were familiar features of the education landscape. In recent years, however, all that has changed. Community education has been seriously depleted.

Given the significance of schools in children's lives this presents a serious challenge to the theme of children and communities. If there is not the political will nationally to promote community education, if there is not the space in the school curriculum to address questions about community, then there is a danger of the community aspects of children's growth and development being unsupported by educational skills and resources – schools, outreach, youth centres, etc.

At the same time the realities of many deprived communities must place a question mark against 'informal' education in community settings. Fear of crime, violence and social unrest are too dominant. Unless detached youth work and informal education programmes aimed at children and young people are undertaken with the support and active co-operation of the institutions (local education authorities, schools) and the community (community centres, tenants' associations, etc.), they are unlikely to succeed. It is as if the ways in which schools relate to their surrounding neighbourhoods and in which they themselves can exist as communities have to be relearnt. Educational and social conditions have changed so radically since the more idealistic period of community education (1960s and 1970s) that a new legitimacy for children and community in the educational context has to be established. Practice models and a language appropriate to the 1990s have to be developed.

This is the assumption behind both chapters in this part of the book. Rupert Prime's description of how a London school developed links with the community through a number of services and programmes is working on a well-established theme. In this

Part 3 Education

Historically, education can lay claim to being the professional sector with the strongest roots in the community. Community schools, community service – community education in general – were familiar features of the education landscape. In recent years, however, all that has changed. Community education has been seriously depleted.

Given the significance of schools in children's lives this presents a serious challenge to the theme of children and communities. If there is not the political will nationally to promote community education, if there is not the space in the school curriculum to address questions about community, then there is a danger of the community aspects of children's growth and development being unsupported by educational skills and resources – schools, outreach, youth centres, etc.

At the same time the realities of many deprived communities must place a question mark against informal education in community settings. Fear of crime, violence and social unrest are too dominant. Unless detached youth work and informal education programmes aimed at children and young people are undertaken with the support and active co-operation of the institutions (local education authorities, schools) and the community (community centres, tenants' associations, etc.) they are unlikely to succeed.

It is as if the ways in which schools relate to their surrounding neighbourhoods and in which they themselves can exist as communities have to be relearnt. Educational and social conditions have changed so radically since the more idealistic period of community education (1960s and 1970s) that a new legitimacy for children and community in the educational context has to be established. Practice models and a language appropriate to the 1990s have to be developed.

This is the assumption behind both chapters in this part of the book. Rupert Prime's description of how a London school developed links with the community through a number of services and programmes is working on a well-established theme. In this case, however, it is cast in the context of changed educational assumptions and less certain societal values. The community activities and programmes documented in the chapter may not by themselves appear to be original, but when placed in the context of a densely populated inner-city area their effectiveness can be appreciated. The multi-racial nature of the school's catchment area is evident and the reader will be interested to compare Rupert Prime's assumptions about black–white relations with those contained in the chapter by Kanchan Jadeja in Part 1.

The contribution of Rachel Hodgkin is concerned with the other side of the school–community coin. She takes as her focus the school defined as a community. This, too, is a theme with a rich history but the author sets out clearly the reasons why, in the 1990s, children's rights to participation in school decision-making, as well as their rights to be consulted on anti-bullying strategies, have to be reasserted. Her arguments for taking seriously the school as a community are encapsulated in her discussion of children with special needs, namely the value that their integration within school has for children without disabilities and for the health of the school as a community.

Both chapters have a practical focus and cover only a small part of the education–community agenda but they may help to bring back into centre stage this crucially important subject. There is a need for a searching debate, not the suppressed agonising of teachers, parents and community leaders about how best to encourage children to play a part in community life. Children have a right to that kind of involvement. It is also a very shortsighted adult world which denies children opportunities to prepare themselves to become responsible adults in the sense that they commit themselves to working for creative, tolerant communities.

6 School and Community Links

Rupert Prime

Introduction – The School and its Environment

Clissold Park school (11- to 16-year-olds) is situated in a predominantly working-class community in north London. The community experiences many of the features of disadvantage in Britain's inner cities. For example, 35 per cent of the school population come from one-parent families – the mother being the parent in all but a few cases. The approximate racial mix is 40 per cent indigenous population (mainly English and Irish), 30 per cent Afro-Caribbean (mostly British by birth), 10 per cent from the Indian subcontinent, 10 per cent Greek and Turkish Cypriot, 5 per cent African origin and others, mainly Vietnamese, 5 per cent.

High-rise estate flats, terraced houses and owner-occupied dwellings exist in equal proportions throughout the community, and light and service industries provide employment to a small proportion of the community; unemployment has always been relatively high.

The current, though unestablished, view is that some 90 per cent of the population has had some form of contact with the police. Furthermore, it is generally accepted, and there is adequate pragmatic evidence to support this, that relationships between the races and cultures are precarious. The number of students moving into the sixth form and/or pursuing further and higher education, compared with the number in other divisions in the education authority, is markedly low.

To the optimistic observer and educationist this situation was one of profound challenge; one in which the school's role was vital, perhaps crucial.

In addition to the well-rehearsed and conventional objectives of any school, many staff shared the view that there were equally compelling objectives for schools within this particular geo-

graphical complex, namely, as far as possible to educate adult
members in the community and to develop in pupils: first, a
healthy respect for and an appreciation of local cultural diversity;
second, the foundation for an ability to participate intelligently
in decisions within their community; and third, a capacity for
objective thinking, thinking which is untrammelled by miscon-
ceptions.

The achievement of these objectives depended essentially on
the close relationship between the school and the community as
well as on the effectiveness of the outreach programmes and
measures devised by the school. Accordingly, the partnership
between the school and the community was not an embellishment of the school's normal curriculum but rather a genuine
activity, the approach to which required the same intellectual rigour
and administrative support as did other normal school
programmes. Aims of community programmes were agreed and
clarified and expressed in operational terms, success criteria
determined, time limits set and resources made available to
support planning, implementation and review.

Staff, school governors and pupils (mainly years 8 to 11) were
informed of the purposes of the project. To this end, the headteacher chaired a small committee of school governors, teaching
staff and sixth form students to consider a number of activities
that the school and the rest of the community could pursue
jointly. It was during these discussions that we, almost belatedly,
recognised that the school-keeping staff – generally the caretakers
– had a crucial role to play in the success of our enterprise, and
it was only after protracted but useful discussions and argument
with them that their support was harnessed.

Our proposed programme was laid before the local authority
education committee. Six months later the school received a
'one-off' payment of £5,555 (further funding was provided subsequently) in support of the project. An edited version of our
submission to the local authority was sent to local organisations
and institutions (for example, the police, banks, hospitals,
newspaper office, home for elderly people, library, shopkeepers,
college for further education) to ask for further financial support,
to inform them about the project, and to ask for their advice and
comments. This exercise brought in £2,785. It was not surprising
that the degree of enthusiasm for our project varied between
institutions and agencies, but in view of the nature of support
promised and the observations made by many in the community,

we on the committee were persuaded and encouraged to modify some of our intentions – a classic example of the community 'advising' the school.

Co-ordination and adequate supervision of the project necessitated the appointment of a member of staff. On taking up her appointment as school and community co-ordinator she undertook a two-month induction and planning period. This enabled her to find out about projects elsewhere in the country and to advise on timetable adjustments aimed at the structured inclusion of school–community programmes.

A large on-site room which was designated to 'community and school' work – the community centre – was well equipped with facilities for refreshment and communications, e.g. word processors/computers, reproduction booths, a small library (multicultural), comfortable furniture and attractive pictures and paintings. There was ample provision of simple items – pens, pencils, writing paper, posters – and the signs were well sited and in four languages. Everything in the room suggested that a genuine effort was being made to welcome all users. Subsequently, as a result of heavy demand, two adjoining rooms were brought into use. The existence of this accommodation, in my opinion, averted the collapse of many of our programmes.

There were times in the school day when staff were released to undertake non-traditional school work; pupils would be included in school–community projects with an examination content, and outside agencies would be invited into school to educate pupils and teachers. Obviously, the best way forward was to incorporate all these activities into the normal school timetable. This was what early planning enabled us to achieve, and this was what was meant by the earlier observation that community–school projects were not an embellishment tacked on to school activities.

Community Activities and Programmes

There were, of course, many other schools within the community and, quite understandably, pupils and their parents would be expected to demonstrate allegiance to the school of their choice. An expectation, then, that a single school had the capacity to capture the support, contacts and imagination of the whole community was, in our view, over-ambitious and unrealistic. We planned, accordingly, to lower our horizons and to work with and through the pupils and parents of our school and to rely on their efforts to increase the 'catchment' of involvement. Moreover, the school had to make a distinction between on the one hand those programmes and activities which were designed directly to promote the education of the pupils, and on the other those which were designed to 'educate' the community and provide the community with the opportunity of participating in the education of the pupils. This distinction was particularly necessary in view of our belief that the concept of 'community links' had the potential to develop into a technology of its own and to float dangerously clear of other considerations, i.e. at the expense of the personal, social and educational development of all pupils.

As teachers, we had a specific responsibility not to embark on any venture, however attractive, which was likely to prejudice pupils' development and the delivery of education. Teachers can never be precise about 'outcomes'; accordingly, adequate and regular monitoring was built into the programme to ensure that pupils' education was not compromised.

After much debate we decided to use the local press, posters, notice boards and personal letters to publicise and extend an invitation to the 'Inauguration of the Community Centre' – years later many staff and members still refer to the ICC. On the day music, food, films, talks and pupils' work, including dance, acrobatics and modelling were all part of the experience. Those who attended were asked to provide their name and address.

Given our reservations noted above concerning the catchment area, we were surprised to discover that more than 25 per cent of those who attended had had no connection whatever with the school, and this discovery served to remind us that there was always a residual section of the community which, given the right incentive and appropriate conditions, would 'cross the floor'.

I will describe some of the activities and projects under two headings, curricular and extra-curricular. This distinction is based less on content and more on the time of day that the exercise was undertaken.

Curricular Activities

All pupils studying English, social studies, commerce, sociology and child care were required, for examination purposes, to undertake a relevant course-work project over a period of two academic years. Whereas most pupils traditionally relied on the material gathered from books and journals, our pupils were encouraged to supplement the traditional sources with experiences and examples they had encountered within the community. These experiences were not to be the random examples and conclusions drawn from poorly constructed questionnaires. They were instead to be the product of a systematic collection of detail. Accordingly, pupils worked alongside an employee in the respective 'agency', and observed and documented their findings. They learned to handle material in books which did not correspond with their experience 'on the job', and to take responsibility for their own learning, e.g. where desirable and practicable, students arranged additional visits to the agency outside school hours, sometimes during school holidays.

It was the responsibility of the School and Community Co-ordinator to negotiate and organise these links, which necessitated the simultaneous release of 180 pupils at a given time, fortnightly. This was no easy task. Not all managers were willing to accept pupils in their workplace. Some, in our view, exaggerated the local difficulties which pupils might generate, but many of those who co-operated were impressed by, and appreciative of, the systematic way in which realism was being injected into pupils' education. I deal later with subsidiary reasons for their support.

Most teachers feel that finding meaningful placements for pupils is a time-consuming and traumatic undertaking. However, because most of our pupils had established links within the community, the time spent allocating pupils to appropriate workplaces was significantly reduced. It also followed that from the pupils' point of view 'work experience' was not merely a traditional exercise or incidental activity, it was part and parcel of a relevant and continuous learning experience.

The following are some examples of the projects and activities undertaken:

1. Policing in Communities

This project, the only one undertaken by all years 9 and 10 pupils, consisted of a series of talks and discussions with the local constabulary. It was a sensitive activity – it has already been noted that, without apportioning blame, many members of the community had had unfortunate contact with the police – and could have degenerated into 'let's get the police' sessions. Initially, the discussions were always chaired by a member of staff with strict rules of conduct in force, e.g. no speaker to be interrupted however much pupils disagreed with what was being said. Fortunately, the officers always came well prepared and demonstrated an awareness of, and responsiveness to, pupils' sensitivities.

The topics covered included the process of selection and training of the police, preparation and production of evidence, compensation to victims of crime/violence, the police and minority groups, complaints against the police, and community support. These topics were supported by exposure to technology in use in the force, visits to relevant places, such as police hostels and Scotland Yard, and mock trials.

With the passage of time a marked degree of trust replaced suspicion. At the end of a normal session teachers witnessed unprompted discussions between members of the force and the pupils, and noticed the extent to which pupils began to rely on the officers for support in the preparation of material for their project. The replacing of a large discussion group with small workshops was a direct and satisfying consequence of the build-up of trust. A number of teachers whose non-teaching period coincided with these sessions chose to attend them and offered to assist.

Most of the staff had felt considerable professional discomfort regarding the inclusion of this project in the community links programme; it was there at the headteacher's insistence and supported by his undertakings and promises. As it turned out, events did not justify staff's pessimism, not because of any inherent virtue in the project, but essentially because the adults in charge displayed sensitivity at the planning stage and efficiency and professionalism at the point of delivery. There was a general feeling that the benefit to pupils and staff outweighed the 'pain' endured at the planning stage.

2. Teaching Adults to Read and Write

For this project groups of no more than ten pupils undertook to teach adults (the number in the teaching group always matched the number of pupils) to read and, depending on progress, to write. Many questions had to be addressed. How do we locate and encourage non-readers to participate? Given the multi-cultural mix in the community, what books would be appropriate and how do we get hold of them? How should we cope with any embarrassment caused by the generation gap? In the event of failure are we qualified to help non-readers manage their distress, and would failure intensify the problem, i.e. make future learning more difficult? It was important to consider these questions, and the pupils needed and received the support of teachers as well as adults who taught in the nearby voluntary teaching adult unit. The parents of pupils were the obvious starting point, and the head-teacher used an assembly to explain to the school what the pupils hoped to achieve by the project.

The 30 pupils involved had a group of 43 adults (in only seven cases was English the first language) to choose from. The teachers had responsibility to assist pupils in monitoring and document-ing progress, assessing and documenting their personal contribution to the work and preparing for the next 'lesson'.

Pupils experienced pride: 'When I taught people as old as my mum to read I felt I was doing something special for the community.' But they encountered difficulty in coping with failure or what in their view was 'slow progress', and there was always the risk, as they themselves discovered, that their own anxiety to succeed would get in the way of the self-confidence of those being taught.

My personal view, based purely on hindsight, was that this project was a difficult undertaking in spite of the 65 per cent success recorded. It had more to do with the school's wish to reach the widest possible audience than with pupils' involvement in the community. It was the only activity which was not repeated.

3. Homes for Elderly People

Those pupils who worked on this project became very attached to the 'elderly person' with whom they worked and supported. The main idea was to give pupils every opportunity to acquaint themselves with and, where practicable, assist in the measures taken to improve the quality of life of elderly people. The pupils visited at least once weekly – many pupils spent much of their own time comforting and helping. They might choose to read poetry, play musical instruments or engage the elderly person in conversation. Many pupils could not be certain that the stories they were told about 'what happened when I was little' were authentic, though many of them would contend that here they learned a great deal more about the history of their community than they did from their text books.

The particular home for elderly people was in its tenth year and catered for a multi-racial group. In the words of one of the pupils, 'it came as a shock to me to see all the English food on every plate and hear only English songs played and see only English folk-dancing'. This was only one of several observations which led to significant changes in service provision.

But the project was not always smooth and comfortable. In our view, far too many pupils had to cope with grief consequent on the death of their 'client', to whom they had become attached. One pupil made the following observation: 'At first I was happy and it was great working in the old people's home; they used to tell us about Stoke Newington when they were little. The books miss many things out. But when the first man died I was sad and did not eat for days. He was my friend and I will miss him.' Managing grief was never an intended outcome, and was well beyond a teacher's competence, and so every effort had to be made to provide pupils with external support. We have since agonised over the retention of this project and relied subsequently on pupil feedback. The project has been retained but with a variety of contingency measures in place.

4. School Assembly

In many multi-cultural schools, assembly has been reduced to the unconvincing utterance of platitudes, or a series of unco-ordinated chatter about the world in which we live, or a feeble attempt to provide moral instruction by means of a disjointed selection of unlikely events: what should I do on finding £5,000 in the park? We came to recognise that there was a reservoir of talent in the community that we could use to advantage. Representatives of various religious cultures were brought together to discuss the ways in which they could contribute to school assemblies. The first three meetings were used, by some, to attack the education system which was failing minorities. But once statements of condemnation of, for example, the 'racist nature of the system' were put on one side, we were able to address the task with vigour. What emerged in the end was a quarterly/termly assembly programme reflecting important religious feast days and festivals, without sacrificing moral content and relevance. In time, pupils were able to hold sensible discussions on cultural aspects of religious practices, prophets, sources of morality and so forth.

The extensive block planning allowed those in charge of assembly to use modern technology to support their effort and hold the attention of staff and pupils. Assembly was no longer 'something that the headteacher told the pupils at a certain time each day' but an activity involving staff and pupils alike. The general view among staff was that our predisposition to emphasise cultural differences was being replaced by a recognition of similarities as well as an appreciation of cultural differences.

5. School-based Workshops

We organised fortnightly workshops in co-operation with the social services department, rehabilitation centres and voluntary agencies within the community and/or released our resources for their use. The target groups were, in general, parents, teachers from schools in the community and our sixth form students. A small fee was charged. We focused on the police and the community, law and order, child abuse, drug abuse, issues of race, children and solvents. A wide press coverage was always guaranteed.

The workshop dealing with 'issues of race and culture' received more press coverage than did the others and one topic in particular – language in a multi-cultural society – drew extensive editorial comments. It was agreed, for example, that in the context of a multi-cultural society 'tolerance' was a condescending term implying feelings of superiority. To many, the remark 'we are willing to tolerate you' was deeply offensive. It is not my intention to develop the argument, but rather to remind readers that unintended outcomes seemed always to lie just beneath the surface of our endeavours. These workshops became self-financing and made a significant impact on the community.

6. Assessment and Marking of Pupils' Work

Every teacher, at some point in his/her career, must have clashed with a parent on some aspect of a child's work or performance: the marking was unfair, the work was a waste of precious time, or some other difference between parents' and teachers' expectations.

Some of these parents were professional artists, computer analysts, poets, joiners, chemists, so why not muscle in on their competence? We decided to invite a group of parents to come into school to participate in the assessment of pupils' work, and hold discussions on it. This exercise revealed that teachers and parents were influenced by different criteria. Some teachers readily admitted that their assessment was often determined by what they felt the pupil was capable of and not what the pupil actually did, which might explain the discrepancy between teachers' assessment of expected examination grades and the grade or standard of performance at the examination proper.

Extra-curricular Activities

The school has an enviable array of electrical, mechanical and scientific equipment and a superb gymnasium well equipped with body-building and weight-lifting facilities, all of which remained idle from 5.30 p.m. until 9.30 a.m. the following day and all through the weekend. The same was true of the large building and extensive playing areas. This, to us, was an unacceptable and avoidable waste in a community with high unemployment and inadequate leisure facilities.

On the other hand, our tennis courts needed resurfacing and remarking and three public roads – one of which was a busy high road – bordered the school grounds and the amount of debris which pedestrians deposited on the premises was a constant bone of contention between the headteacher and the school-keeping staff. In all these areas the local education authority seemed unable to assist. At the same time, members of the community were demanding that extra parking facilities be made available to meet the heavy demand on Saturdays, and that several unused green areas be converted into periodic trading areas.

We formed a small committee to consider 'more efficient use of resources and improvement to the school environment through community links'. The committee comprised school teachers, two local councillors, parents, heads of voluntary associations, market traders and co-opted members representing several interest groups. In setting up the curricular focused programme of activities, the school had acquired several important contacts and outreach skills; this library of competence was now at its disposal to assist in establishing the extra curricular programme of activities.

1. Saturday Morning Club

Children aged 11 to 15 years from any school in the area were enroled to join one class for 18 weeks. They could, if they wished, attend two different classes within a school year.

The number of pupils, approximately 330, who attended varied little and, because of the high demand for places, the period of time spent in some classes was reduced to nine weeks. There were no general criteria for admission to the club, nor did the co-ordinator enquire into the behavioral record or background of any applicant. A 'wish to attend' was sufficient to merit genuine consideration. Of the 330 pupils in sessional attendance about 120 attended the 'parent' school.

The teachers for the club came from the 'parent' school, teachers from other local schools and, provided that they had the appropriate skills and stood up to rigorous scrutiny, the parents of school-aged children as well as adults with no direct or indirect link with education. Since remuneration was low, many in the latter group regarded 'teaching children within the community' as a neat and rewarding way to put something back into the community.

Chemistry and physics were notable absences in the early stage. These subjects were regarded as high-risk areas and were not included in the 'extra curricular' programme until suitably qualified teachers were available. This precaution was taken in spite of the declaration signed by parents of participating pupils absolving teachers from a number of liabilities.

Qualified and unqualified teachers often worked in tandem, supporting and learning from one another, while pupils from different schools mingled freely and easily with one another. Although the population as a whole was heterogeneous there were few complaints or evidence of disorder, disruption or the 'problems' normally associated with schools and schooling.

2. Evening Clubs

Evening clubs represented a further attempt to optimise the use of school premises and equipment. As it turned out the school gymnasia, the tennis courts, business studies, art and word processing/computers were the only areas 'hired' out for a reasonable financial return four evenings a week. In order to keep necessary supervision to a minimum no more than three classes were allowed to run simultaneously.

Small clubs and voluntary and self-help groups accordingly joined forces to rationalise the demand for and use of the 'updated equipment'. There were, of course, occasions when the regular school teachers felt aggrieved at the abuse of equipment but the consensus was that in addition to the financial advantage to the school, the large number of people (approximately 360 weekly) using the equipment was a significant advantage to the community.

3. The Garden

New measures had to be taken to improve the appearance of the school and a parent's idea that the area be transformed into a garden was adopted. There seemed always to be that parent who knew someone – often outside the catchment area – with special skills at the disposal of the community. The well-established lines of communication were set in motion and very few in the community would not have known that the school intended to take action to rid its perimeter of debris.

For the first time teachers had to take a back seat or, to be less irreverent, had to lead from behind. The design of the landscape – the location and size of tubs, the distribution of plants, shrubs and flowers, the selection of soil, all these were features beyond the competence of most teachers. It took the gang (so they wished to be called) four consecutive weekends to complete the task. The local press now took over with photographs and extensive coverage of the effort. The caption 'Now keep your rubbish out' was short and effective.

The names of contributing firms were strategically sited (by way of public thanks and as a form of advertisement) as well as the request 'No rubbish please'. All the labour and most of the materials were donated to the school, and so the financial cost to the school for this vast undertaking was minimal.

4. Tennis Courts and Play Areas

These areas were in a bad state of disrepair, and the financial cost of repair was beyond our resources. But could we again approach the community for support? We did – this time for advice on use. The community response was considerable. There was advice ranging from off-street parking free of charge to the community only, to weekly exhibitions and mobile library, and a site for inoculation. There were offers of free labour and material and planning. The suggestion that the site should be used extensively during school holidays generated favourable editorial comment from the south London press, and discussion in the council chamber.

Armed with the achievements of our school–community links we managed to obtain additional financial support from the LEA to meet the entire cost of resurfacing the tennis courts and play areas, parts of which were marked as parking bays. These parking bays, open to the community on Saturdays and, on occasion, throughout the weekend for parking and boot sales, went some way towards satisfying community needs. By carefully managed extension of public use of the parking bays we had a regular and reliable source of income through which we financed many school-community links in later years.

5. Use of the Community Centre

It was common knowledge throughout the community that 'if you went to that large school anytime during the day, someone would always be there to help you with your reply to the gas or electric company, or with your reading or teach you to use the telephone'. One Bangladeshi woman wished to know why in England one would normally say 'bye' before replacing the receiver. 'It is like "Roger and Out"' was a pupil's apt reply. To many, the school was the place to go to have problems of communication solved, questions about voting or about education in other schools answered.

Council officers had mixed feelings with regard to those non-English speaking residents who wished to meet the housing officer in our community centre because 'the school would honour any promise made to provide an interpreter'. The meeting was convened as requested. Subsequently, a debate 'To what extent should the Church be involved in national politics?' was replaced by the debate 'To what extent should the school be involved in local politics?' But the school was neither taking a political stance nor advising on political preferences or decisions, it was doing no more than providing the facilities for decisions to be reached or discussions to take place.

Reflections

School governors, parents and their friends, and sometimes pupils played a key role in contacting or identifying pockets of resources within the community: they were familiar with the resource terrain, had relatives and friends who were liberal resource holders and they would have had recent contact with community-minded groups or individuals or recently retired people with time, energy and goodwill to spare. Their 'outreach' potential was far superior to that of the professionals (teachers) many of whom lived outside the catchment area. For us the clear learning point was that while dependence on professional acumen might be necessary, it could never be sufficient in our 'outreach' effort. We had to work with the knowledgeable sector of the community in order to reach the wider community.

Readers may find it strange that, notwithstanding the general shortage of resources, the school was able to find additional resources, both financial and human, to support its community links programme; how did the school 'manage' its requests and appeal for resources? All schools within the LEA had to provide the LEA, annually, with a curriculum analysis on the basis of which the school could make demands for additional, or the reallocation of existing, resources. The curriculum analysis normally identified all curriculum activities, number of classes and/or teaching groups, their size, frequency of lessons, etc. By skilful and defensible manipulation of the curriculum analysis the school was able to support its resource demands. Furthermore, the headteacher encouraged the divisional inspector to participate in discussion on the community links programme and to advise on technical matters. His intention was not to 'purchase' the inspectoral support but to guarantee that inspectoral representation was based on genuine acquaintance with the activity and its resource implications.

The Staff

The commitment of both the teaching and school-keeping staff to supporting the school's involvement with the community was crucially important. In order to assist the personal and professional development of the former group, programmes were often considered not only in terms of content for pupils but also in terms of teaching and organisational skills. Also it was very apparent at school–community meetings that the contribution of school-keeping staff was respected. Had we not recognised their importance, our efforts to establish school–community links would have collapsed.

The Police

The mention of the phrase 'police in schools' was enough to precipitate emotional and unhelpful comment, and yet to have excluded the police from the project would, in our view, have been a grave blunder. Several issues troubled us and generated considerable discomfort, in particular whom to include or exclude, when to approach the press, parents and the LEA (which was not always supportive of school–community links), and how much reliance to place on pupils and their ability to handle sensitive issues.

The Press

It is often claimed that the local press shy away from reporting on educational matters which are not sensational. We were all concerned that the adverse publicity on any aspect of our school–community link programme, or the insensitive reporting of any accident, was enough to jeopardise the success of the entire programme. But press coverage seemed crucial to the success of our venture – the bold photographs and provocative captions reached many households and it was expedient, therefore, that we sought press support.

We believed that we secured a promise of sensitive reporting by presenting a meaningful package: clearly stated operational aims, structured programmes, strategic timing of press contacts, adequate briefing of the press (this was best achieved through the attendance of a press reporter at planning meetings) and their discretion to edit appropriately.

Black Pupils in the Community

The placement of black pupils highlighted the prejudices which several managers harboured, e.g. a reluctance to have 'blacks' on their staff 'because they are black' or because 'their very presence would have an adverse effect on sales'. At the same time many black pupils were reluctant to work in institutions because they would be exposing themselves to avoidable prejudice and discrimination. The school responded by developing a strategy to manage this twin dilemma.

Briefly, a meeting attended by several managers or their representative, teachers and pupils confronted these issues and fears. It was reassuring to pupils to hear several employers express the view that the very presence of black people on their staff was an asset in that it would help staff acquire communication and linguistic skills and other competences in dealing with a section of their clientele. All participating firms were offered free advertising space in the school brochure, the school handbook and the school programme of its extra-curricular activities. The school, for the first time, paid for additional space in the local paper to report this meeting and subsequent to this report many more managers requested inclusion in the programme.

It has been demonstrated that within the community there exist many pockets of human and material resources which can be channelled into schools, and that the community can in turn look to schools for support of some of its weaker members. It has also been demonstrated that pupils of every race can be taught, at an early age, to exploit the resources within their community. Through systematic and guided exposure to institutions and services within the community, they can be helped to acquire a sense of responsibility as well as those sensitivities which can enhance and enrich their educational experience, and the quality of life within the school.

School within the Community

Every school has the potential to converse with a section of the community, but in large conurbations no one school could successfully converse with the 'whole' community. It is the combined efforts of all schools which is likely to involve the 'whole' community. Of course, the individual efforts of schools within the community context are, by their very nature, independent and separate; they could be oppressive and could clash (e.g. where many schools make separate demands on the community for its resources). As the number of schools in school–community links network increases, the need for schools to find ingenious ways to avoid overbearing demand and counter-productive clashes will increase proportionately. School–community wide links are possible to the extent that schools are willing to co-operate with one another in the school–community links programmes.

The School

In developing our programme we wanted to test to the full the scope for community involvement in education. At the same time we were determined to find a variety of ways whereby the school could become a resource for the community. In following the latter route, we were aware of the danger of the school being drawn into a wide variety of community activities. 'If they (the teachers) are successful at all, the needs of the neighbourhood for health, housing, employment and other services will be found to impinge directly on their tasks' (Cosin, 1977). I believe we avoided this trap for two main reasons: the commitment to the development of school–community links by all levels of staff; and an approach which favoured an emphasis on rational planning processes and the achievement of clear but limited objectives as opposed to ad hoc and partial initiatives.

The Role of the Headteacher

It is probably an error of judgement or excessive humility not to have elaborated on the essential role of the headteacher. It may be enough to say that unless the project has the full support of the headteacher it is doomed to failure. Within two years of my moving on to another headship, interest in the school–community project began to wane, the traditional forms of learning and experiencing reasserted themselves, and contacts with the community dwindled. This is not a comment on the competence of the new headteacher or the outgoing headteacher but rather an attempt to highlight the importance of the role of the head-teacher in an activity which is important but to which no professional imperative is attached.

Reference

Cosin, B.R., Dale, I.R., Esland, G.M., Mackinnon, D. and Swift, D.R. eds. (1977) *School and Society: A Sociological Reader*, 2nd edition, Milton Keynes: Open University, p. 65.

7 Schools and Community

Rachel Hodgkin

This chapter is not about how schools relate to their surrounding communities but about how they operate as communities in their own right, and the extent to which children are active participants in the running of that community.

There are a few schools operating in the UK which give pupils genuine control over what they learn, how they are taught and how the school operates (for example the Sands School in Devon or A.S. Neill's Summerhill in Suffolk).

These are, unavoidably, independent schools since the government has made it impossible for such rights to be introduced in the maintained sector. The National Curriculum now specifies the fine detail of what is to be taught in over 70 per cent of the day in maintained schools and requires pupils to be tested at regular intervals. The government has also abolished the right of pupils to become school governors and has taken other prescriptive steps, forbidding the pursuit of 'partisan political activities by any of those registered pupils at the school who are junior pupils' and empowering the school governors to ban sex education (Education (No. 2) Act 1986, sections 15, 44 and 18). All these steps militate against freedom of thought and self-determination by pupils.

Revealingly, head teachers are required by law to seek measures to ensure pupils have a 'proper regard for authority' (section 22 of the Education (No. 2) Act 1986), and you can be sure 'a proper regard' does not mean questioning or challenging the validity of this 'authority'.

In recent political debates the term 'child-centred education' has become one of abuse. The government claims that its reforms have made education 'parent-centred', so for example as part of its Citizen's Charter there is a parents' charter in education. Its critics say that parents' rights are an illusion and the truth is that

122

education is now 'Secretary of State-centred'. Children are completely marginal to this debate: none of the political parties recognises that it is pupils, not parents, who are the primary consumers of education. There is no children's charter.

Why is it important for pupils to have rights of participation and freedom of expression? One simple reason is that schools work better if the pupils are respected and given responsibilities. As the 1989 Committee of Inquiry into Discipline in Schools stated:

> We have suggested that pupils learn more in school than they are taught. They also learn from messages carried by the way in which the school is run and the relationships between people in it. Our impression is that, in schools with a negative atmosphere, pupils learn to see themselves as irresponsible beings who must be contained and controlled at all times. Our evidence suggests that pupils tend to live up, or down, to teachers' expectations. (Elton Report, 1989, 6.3, p. 142)

Taking a comparison with the management of industry, it is now recognised that it is not enough simply to reward the workforce with adequate salaries. Productivity and job satisfaction increase if workers feel that they are respected, have delegated responsibilities and some say in the running of the company. These principles can easily be applied to schools, and can be shown to be as effective.

Another reason why pupil participation is important is that the exercise of rights is educative – children will learn to be responsible members of society only if they practice responsibility.

Over and above these arguments is the fact that children are now, under international law, entitled to far greater rights in school. Article 12 of the UN Convention on the Rights of the Child provides:

1. States Parties shall assure to the child who is capable of forming his or her own views the right to express these views freely *in all matters affecting the child*, the view of the child being given due weight in accordance with the age and maturity of the child.

2. For this purpose, the child shall in particular be provided with the opportunity to be heard in any judicial *and administrative proceedings* affecting the child, either directly or through a representative or an appropriate body, in a manner consistent with the procedural rules of national law.

Before the UK ratified the Convention the various government departments were consulted about its implications and given the opportunity to enter reservations to particular articles which would absolve the government from a duty to abide by its provisions. No reservations were entered regarding education, and when the Convention was ratified the Department for Education issued a press notice from the Education Minister which claimed that all the Convention's articles relating to education were being met in full, indeed exceeded.

Characteristically what the Department for Education had done was to look only at the Convention's articles specifically addressing education, without considering how the more general principles, like article 12, might relate to education.

The gap between the education world and the services dealing with children is at its widest over this question of children's right to be heard and to participate in decision making. Under the Children Act 1989 courts and social services have to ascertain and give due consideration to the views of children (uniquely in education law, the Act also places a similar duty on the supervisor of an education supervision order). The 1985 House of Lords ruling in the Gillick case transformed children's rights to determine decisions, establishing that children under the age of 16 had rights to consent to treatment if they were deemed to have 'sufficient understanding', and that parents' rights to control their children dwindled as their child grew older. This principle was accepted and put into operation by health practitioners.

While the Education Act 1994 was passing through Parliament, a number of attempts were made to introduce provisions to give children article 12 rights in schools. These have been some of the ministerial responses:

> The question has just arisen why, if such a provision was good enough for the Children Act 1989, it is not good enough for the Education Bill – a fair question. The answer is that the (Children) Act ranges much more widely on welfare issues, inter-personal relations and the child's existence in a social environment, whereas the Bill deals with more strictly educational matters. It is at least arguable that there is a difference between taking full account of a young person's attitudes and responses in a social and welfare context and asking the child to make a judgement, utter an opinion or give a view on his or her educational requirements . . .' (Hansard, House

of Commons Education Bill Committee Stage, 26 January 1993, col. 1108)

On a similar amendment at a later stage the Minister, Eric Forth, said he was going to refrain from actually calling the idea of consulting pupils 'dotty' (as had some MPs) but would condemn it as 'politically correct'. He dismissed the amendment as:

> too all-embracing and tries to go too far. It attempts to include all age groups of pupils in schools, which is not only too ambitious, but, in many circumstances would be absurd and unworkable. (Hansard, House of Commons Education Bill Committee Stage, 9 February 1993, col. 1515)

Then in the House of Lords the government was challenged directly on its failure to implement the UN Convention in schools. Lord Henley, on behalf of the government, replied:

> My advice is that there is no conflict between the Education Bill and the UN Convention. Article 12 of the Convention states that the child shall in particular be provided with the opportunity to be heard in any judicial or administrative proceedings affecting the child. We believe that the Children Act should cater for that. Therefore, I believe that my noble friend's amendment is unnecessary to bring us within the ambit of article 12. (Hansard, House of Lords, 20 April 1993, col. 1547)

How extraordinary, and how typical, are these remarks!

The underlying implication is that whereas the consideration of children's views might be appropriate for courts and social workers it is inappropriate and irrelevant where education is concerned. But article 12 refers to 'all matters' and 'any administrative proceeding' affecting the child. Education is obviously such a matter, as are all the formal administrative proceedings operating within the education system such as school choice, special education proceedings, exclusion appeals, etc. in which under 18 year olds have no representative rights.

The government's dismissal appears to rest on two assumptions. The first is a common misunderstanding which mixes up children's right to be heard with giving them a right to make decisions, and which suggests that a right to be heard means that children *must* express an opinion. Article 12 does not give children rights to self-determination, only rights to have their views – if they wish to express them – considered on matters affecting them. This is of course common sense: any professional will confirm that the child's attitude towards a decision is crucial to a successful outcome. Even if you override children's wishes it is essential to know them.

Secondly there seems to be an assumption that education is in some way different to social work, court cases or health care. It cannot be that education is more complicated or serious – nothing could be more difficult or serious than some of the life decisions judges, social workers and doctors have to make about children. It is the inherently condescending and compulsory nature of education that sets it apart from these other disciplines. No one proposes that the views of culprits should be considered on the nature of their punishment (except perhaps to find out what they would like least and then apply it) and I suspect that education as administered in most schools is more akin to punishment than its practitioners would care to acknowledge.

Nonetheless, despite the authoritarian centralisation of education, despite the effect the cuts have had on extracurricular initiatives, despite the low morale, there is exciting work being done in many schools giving genuine recognition to children's rights to participate in the running of schools and their own education. The point is that, unfortunately, all these initiatives are swimming against the tide of current education policy. Certainly attempts to introduce child-initiated curricula have been more or less scuppered by the National Curriculum. The following examples of existing good practice therefore focus not on the content of education but on the running of schools. Three aspects are considered – pupil participation, bullying and the integration of children with special needs.

Pupil Participation

Now that pupil governors are prohibited in law (although some schools still co-opt them on to the governing body as observers), the commonest method of involving the student body in decision making about the school is through school councils. Of course the simple existence of a school council does not guarantee pupils any genuine rights or involvement, as the Elton Committee points out:

> Our impression is that, where they [school councils] exist, pupils are likely to make responsible use of them. We would,

however, discourage the creation of token councils. If it becomes clear to pupils that staff are taking no notice of their views, the council is likely to become a liability rather than an asset. Setting up a council that works involves a commitment to staff to listen to what pupils are saying and to take their views seriously. We believe that commitment is worth making. (Elton Report, 1989, 6.9, pp. 143–44)

But it is not surprising that school councils have emerged as the main method of canvassing the views of pupils: representative bodies tend to be the principle vehicle for the exercise of democracy in most societies. The development of children's councils, referred to by Paul Henderson in the Introduction above, is a comparable example.

Some of the more exciting examples of effective school councils are those operating (contrary to Education Ministers' remarks about ages and abilities) in primary schools or special schools. This is Rebecca Matthews, aged ten, of Muswell Hill Primary School, describing how the pupils' council for the junior school had improved the life of the school:

A lot of the complaints coming from the children were about the playground. We were finding that games were being smashed up by football and that there were arguments about space. So the council suggested that an area for football should be marked out and said that balls could only be kicked about in that area, and also that hard balls could not be used. The school council said that each of the four years would have a day on which they could use the area, and made Friday a girls-only football day.

Then there was the quiet area, but it wasn't quiet – people ran in and out all the time, so the school council organised a 'patrol' of children to make sure that it was quiet. We found that the dinner ladies were not really doing anything about complaints made by the children about other children, so we got them to note down the names of naughty children and send them to the head if necessary.

We asked for the outside toilets to be cleaned up and for soft paper not hard and for the water fountains to be repaired. The children thought that there was too much swearing so we agreed a 'no swearing' ban and put up no swearing posters. We also agreed that fruit and vegetables could be eaten in the morning break, but not sweets. Now we are trying to get some picnic tables . . .

The consulting of pupils in special schools is not uncommon, particularly in some of the more enlightened EBD schools (schools for children with emotional and behavioural difficulties). It is uncommon, however, where children with learning difficulties are concerned. When a large new special school opened in 1992 in Darlington (following the amalgamation of three schools for children with severe learning difficulties, moderate learning difficulties and physical disabilities) the staff were determined to involve the children, whatever their disability, in the running of the school. They had hoped to join a network of special schools involved in similar initiatives, but could find no other examples. The deputy headteacher, Dave Johnson, here describes their progress:

> Beaumont Hill School was new with a lot of new staff and we agreed that one of the most important aims would be to enable the students to share in a sense of common ownership of the school. Setting up a student council was one way to achieve this – partly to give them some say in the affairs of the school, a feeling that nothing was written on tablets of stone and they could influence decisions, but also for the educational experience of taking responsibility and having to negotiate and agree issues.
>
> Each class elected two students for the council, and we also thought about how the pupils with very severe learning difficulties should be represented. So far the council has played an active role – for example sorting out the rules to protect students in wheelchairs (keeping to the left in the corridor and so forth), organising the Christmas disco and an anti-litter competition, starting to address the issue of bullying and vandalism. It now has a small budget, money is allocated and any profits from events go to it. The council is such an important part of the school management and the learning of the students that we have shifted it from being held in leisure periods to taking place in time-tabled time.

Not only can the principles of the UN Convention be applied in schools of any age group and any ability, but there is also no limit to the sorts of decision the students can come to grips with.

Here is an extract from an article about a comprehensive, Norham Community School, in North Shields:

> The pupils help decide how the school budget is spent and have a say in what and how they are taught. They have implemented a system of rewards for merit and attendance. Now they are working on plans for an improved sports hall and helping to redesign the playing fields . . .
>
> Instead of having a students' council, where pupils might discuss the school uniform or the state of the lavatories, the pupils at Norham have a management committee, made up of a dozen 15 and 16 year olds, which advises the school governors.
>
> The pupils are also working with the Leisure and Tourism Department at North Tyneside Council in an attempt to extract £350,000 from the Government's City Challenge fund. Staff from the department, and from the Countryside Commission, regularly visit the school to consult pupils about plans for the playing fields.
>
> Some of the school's policies may sound like Sixties liberalism, but the exam pass rates, attendance levels and teacher morale have all improved. 'Praise and encouragement make everyone perform better than a barrage of criticism,' says deputy headteacher, Margaret Stone. 'We asked pupils to comment on the style and content of lessons,' she continues. 'Some of the staff did feel threatened because they were afraid we were allowing pupils to be critical, but many said they would alter their lessons to take account of what the children said.' (Handscomb, the *Independent*, 1992)

Bullying

Some children experience schools as fulfilling and exciting places; most have mixed views, the pluses usually attached to their friends, their favourite subjects and the occasional inspiring teacher, the negatives arising from boring, irrelevant lessons and the lack of freedom and respect. But for a few children school is a living hell. This is because they are bullied, usually by other children but sometimes by teachers. Bullying can be so traumatic that many victims consider themselves scarred for life. Some children even kill themselves.

Several recent suicides of this nature awoke public and media attention to the issue. Some right-wing education pundits held that bullying in schools was a new phenomenon, the result of 1960s' *laissez-faire* whereby teachers declined to enforce standards and so allowed the playground bully to fill the moral vacuum. But anyone educated in the stricter pre- and post-war schools can confirm (if they are being honest) that there was no shortage of bullying – often dismissed as 'part of life' by teachers and sometimes even tacitly condoned by them (such attitudes of course continue today). Nor did old-fashioned penalties stop bullying. School records on corporal punishment, the favourite response to bullying on the lines of give-him-a-taste-of-his-own-medicine, show that the same pupil gets beaten over and over again for bullying: certainly not a deterrent and perhaps an incentive, provoking the bully to take out his humiliation on someone smaller.

Research in Scandinavia in the 1980s discovered that although there were no absolute cures for bullying, certain strategies – in particular the school adopting an anti-bullying policy – did decrease its prevalence. However a massive Norwegian anti-bullying campaign revealed another truth. The three-year project involved all schools being sent a booklet and video, an information sheet for parents and a survey of 600,000 pupils. The evaluation discovered that where schools gave the strategy a high profile the incidence of bullying decreased, but that overall there was an apparent increase of bullying. In other words if you encourage pupils to speak out about bullying you may seem to have more bullying.

In the UK a 'pack' on combatting bullying was prepared in 1992 by the Scottish Council for Research in Education and distributed first to all Scottish schools and then to schools in England and Wales. The pack includes a booklet on practical ideas, management information on drawing up and publicising a policy, and scenarios to use for discussion.

Consulting the pupils is a central part of adopting an anti-bullying strategy. The pack suggests that surveys be conducted – that pupils are asked to write about the school, to consider the procedures for integrating new pupils and for using the curriculum to discuss the issue of bullying, and to 'examine the hidden curriculum; what kinds of messages do the school documents and the school staff give out?'

This pack is carefully worded to be encouraging without being too prescriptive: the government, so willing to prescribe in so many areas, fights shy of dictating to schools on this crucial matter. On the question of 'bully courts', however, the pack is quite inter-

ventionist. These are courts made up of other children, the bully's
'peers', who judge the case and suggest or impose a penalty. At
first sight this might seem attractive to those who believe in
involving children. But the pack makes the following points
about bully courts:

- if the children judge and the teacher observes, the limits of
  'punishment' available have to be pre-defined very strictly. The
  pupils may advocate vengeful measures if given their heads.
- what sort of 'punishment' can be meted out anyway? A punitive
  response can make the problem worse. How sophisticated a
  response can the pupils make? What factors can they take into
  account?
- how will the victim feel? Is the bully court a further humiliation,
  a proof of weakness? You cannot offer bully courts for some victims
  and not for others – or can you?
- if the bullies are a gang, will the bully court make them worse?
  Bully gangs are difficult to handle.
- what will you tell the parents? Parents have to know and agree
  in advance, otherwise problems will arise. Problems may still arise
  if a bully pupil goes home in tears after a court 'hearing'. How
  will the parents react?
- what if the 'punishment' doesn't work? How will the pupils
  react? What can you do? (Scottish Council for Research in
  Education, 1992)

The pack goes on to say that 'This long list of questions arising
may give a more negative picture of bully courts than they
deserve', but the questions do damn such schemes pretty effectively. What is interesting about the objections is that they are
not about problems resulting from the active participation of
children, but about the problems arising from courts and
punishment *per se*. So, for example, the word 'teacher' could be
substituted for the word 'pupils' without unduly distorting the
sense of the passage.

There is no question that for an anti-bullying campaign to be
successful the pupils have to be actively involved – and not just
as a one-off event, but continuously: it is the process not the end
product which is the key issue.

This fact was brought home to one school which had a vigorous
anti-bullying strategy – the Peers School in Oxford. It had bravely
decided to adopt a policy: bravely because if a school announces
it is drawing up a bullying policy it is automatically assumed to

have a bullying problem and, indeed, it may appear to have such a problem in the initial stages when pupils are being encouraged to speak out about their experiences.

The Peers School, in the words of the deputy headteacher Dick Matthews, had to do a lot of groundwork relating to attitudes within the school:

> Everyone has to have achievements recognised, not just good A levels; everyone needs praise and the school needs to welcome all comers. It is very important to recognise that the school is a work-place like Sainsburys: the pupils come to do a job and they have a right to get on with that job without disturbance.

The school conducted surveys, consultations and discussions on bullying. For example an analysis of a year 10 (fourth form) questionnaire showed that more than half the year had both had the experience of being bullied and had bullied themselves.

The results were themselves then used as a discussion paper:

> Why do you think some people get bullied?
> Results mainly centred on being 'different', e.g. race, religion, dress, too brainy, where they live, talking posh, not following the crowd. *Why should being different provoke bullying?* . . .
> Why do some people become bullies?
> Responses said it was mostly done to create some sort of image to be tough or to impress their friends or to look hard. *Who is impressed by this sort of behaviour and why?*
> Many thought that people who were bullies had been bullied themselves. *Why should this be?* . . .
> Why do victims often hide the fact that they are being bullied?
> Responses mainly centred on being afraid that the situation would get worse and embarrassment at being identified as a victim. *If someone is not told, what is going to change?* . . .
> How can you prevent yourself from becoming a victim?
> A wide variety of responses here. Some people concentrated on those victims who had spread rumours and advised them 'to keep their mouths shut'. Others merely said, 'be nice to people?' *Will being nice to people make a difference?* Some responses were very negative, saying that you cannot avoid becoming a victim. *Need this always be true?*

What help do you think can be given to bullies?
Many thoughtful responses here, ranging from 'you can't help them' to 'they need psychiatric help'. Most focused on the need for the bully to understand what he/she is doing. *What would be the outcome of a face to face meeting between the bullies/bully and the victim, with parents and teachers present? What do you think the school should do about bullying?*

On the basis of discussions like these the school published a bullying policy (alongside an agreed code of conduct and a statement of policy on equal opportunities). The policy defined bullying:

Anything that intends to hurt or belittle someone; that makes them feel ashamed, unhappy or afraid . . . if you are part of a group that makes anybody feel ashamed, unhappy or afraid, *you are involved in bullying.*
Excuses will not be accepted.
'I was there but didn't do anything.'
If you did not try to stop it or get help you are partly responsible and therefore involved.
'We were only messing about.'
Was everybody laughing? Did everyone find it funny? Did you stay and help the person who was upset? If not it's bullying!

Pupils are encouraged to speak out – both victims of bullying and those who are aware of it happening – and the leaflet outlines likely consequences (parents always being informed, separate interviewing of bullies, exclusion of bullies if they are preventing someone from gaining an education).

After initial hesitation parents were enthusiastic about the Peers School's approach to the issue. Ironically the school then found that neighbouring schools were adopting the school's written bullying policy without any of the accompanying, and essential, work with the pupils. This had the detrimental effect of devaluing the Peers School policy.

However, the school's deputy head is in favour of there being a legal requirement to have a bullying policy:

If all schools had a policy, they would be less hesitant to talk about bullying knowing that they would not be labelled as 'having a problem' . . . A bullying policy is very easy to write . . . any code of conduct or bullying policy must be generated, discussed and agreed upon by all sections of the school community. It needs to be constantly referred to, seen to be effective and understood by all. This takes time.

The Integration of Pupils with Special Needs

The point I wish to make about this issue is not about the value of integration to children with special needs but about its value to children without disabilities and to the health of a school as a community.

Many parents of disabled children fight hard to have their children educated in mainstream schools, but some, having won the fight, are bitterly disappointed by the outcome. Sometimes this is because the special education provision is under-resourced and so does not meet their child's needs, in short a question of money. But sometimes the parent and child retire, defeated, to a segregated school for social reasons – perhaps because the child has been teased, perhaps just because of the strain of being isolated and friendless.

This is almost entirely the fault of the school. Of course children cannot be forced to be friends, but schools cannot simply sit back and assume that social integration will happen by magic.

The Townsend Church of England Secondary School in St Albans, for example, made sure that when it took on a unit for profoundly deaf children it made huge efforts to ensure that these children were socially integrated. Although they had to attend separate classes on most academic subjects they were integrated for all crafts and sporting lessons as well as all extracurricular activities. More importantly the whole school was taught basic signing, and some children opted for advanced classes. The school had a significant intake of ethnic minority children and was concerned about racial harassment, but discussions with the students quickly revealed that the problem was larger – harassment for 'difference'. The joint staff–student exercise ended in a code Respect for All, posted up in every classroom. It included the words:

> We particularly reject the way that some people abuse others
> because they are richer or poorer, older or younger,
> because they are small or tall, thin or fat,
> because of the colour of their skin,
> because they are male or female,
> because they are a teacher or a pupil,
> because of handicap or personal problems,

because of their looks or what they wear,
because of their likes and dislikes,
because they are popular or unpopular,
because of their ability or lack of ability,
because of nationality or accent.

A lot of work has been done in Canada and the United States, where integration is more advanced, to ensure schools take an active role in planning for social integration – discussing disability with the children and setting up 'friendship circles' to welcome new children (both with and without disabilities). Some similar initiatives have been taken in the UK, for example at the Beckford Primary School in North London. Here a support teacher for Sophia, a girl with Downs Syndrome, records the words of some of Sophia's 'circle of friends':

Alice (the support teacher): There are some teachers who actually think that children like Sophia shouldn't be in ordinary schools; they think she should be in a special school. What do you think of that?

Hannah: I think those teachers should be fired.

Alice: Why do you think that?

Hannah: Because they are really horrible, because if they think that people like Sophia and people similar to her shouldn't be in school, well I think everybody should be in the same school as everybody else. They are the same inside and they just can't see that and they should if they want to be a teacher because they have to care about everybody.

Lauren: And it would really ruin it if she left now because she's made millions of friends at Beckford.

Alexia: She's really got used to them and she really likes them now. If she goes to another school she'll never get on with other people and always think of us.

Steven: Yeah, I know they could be horrible and we wouldn't know.

Alexia: Yeah they might do something really bad to her and like make her keep it a secret . . .

Alice: Do you think she'll be able to go to secondary school when you all go to secondary school?

Alexia: Yes.

Lauren: We'll probably take Sophia with us.

Hannah: Yes, because she's really starting to catch up with us, she's nearly there.

Daniel: She's pulling her act together.
Hannah: Sometimes she's actually better than other people . . .
Alice: Do you think she will have any particular problems?
Hannah: I think she'll have trouble getting people to see that
she's just the same as everybody else. Just getting people to
see that she is nice and things. (Alice Paige-Smith, unpublished)

The world and the media is currently anguished about children
– about their lack of moral values, their materialism and their anti-
social behaviour. Schools are held to be as responsible as parents
for this degeneration, and the National Curriculum Council has
rushed to produce *Spiritual and Moral Development – a Discussion
Paper*. Much is made of what are moral absolutes; the contribution of the compulsory collective act of worship is examined in
detail; teachers are told to act as role models and set firm limits.
But the opportunities offered by schools as micro-communities
for 'citizenship training' (in the words of the Home Secretary) are
scarcely touched upon. The examples given provide hope and
pleasure about the potential of schools; our disapproval should
be directed not towards children but towards the lack of political
will to recognise this potential.

References

Elton Report (1989) *Discipline in Schools*, report of committee of
enquiry, London: Department of Education and Science, HMSO.
Handscomb, Mark (1992) the *Independent*, 30 April.
Paige-Smith, Alice (nd) 'Inside Integration: Sophia at Beckford
School', unpublished.
Scottish Council for Research in Education (1992) *Action Against
Bullying*, Edinburgh: Scottish Education Office.

Part 4 Neighbourhood

In this part of the book the reader has the opportunity to explore a more generalist approach to our theme of children and communities. It is generalist because of the holistic nature of community development, which moves between professions and disciplines and always seeks to relate to the needs and concerns of local people. In any neighbourhood these needs and concerns are diverse and can change rapidly.

A problem arising from the breadth and variety of work at neighbourhood level is the lack of a well-developed vocabulary for understanding the connections between communities, neighbourhoods and children. Furthermore it is apparent that practitioners often face dilemmas of choice because they are pulled between adult and children's agendas. This is of critical importance for agencies and individuals who wish to put children first. Within the following chapters lie vitally important guidance on how to work with children in the neighbourhood context. And that guidance is as much about dialogue between children and adults – about their respective lives, the blockages and connections between the worlds of children and adults – as it is about obtaining resources and facilities for children in neighbourhoods. The chapters are haunted by the elusive search for community, because neighbourhoods hold the possibility of different interest groups – in this case children and adults – agreeing on values which bring people away from obsessive individualism to a culture of sharing, and of the recognition of differences (Etzioni, 1993).

Children and their concerns can be marginalised as a result of adult power. This risk can be heightened when working in the neighbourhood context because of the absence of obvious structures: the community development process, which can be powerful and convincing, can also work against the interests of children. Thus the three chapters raise questions for community workers and others about adult assumptions: how can they work so that the identity and creativity of children receive proper recognition?

This question runs through Craig Russell's material on the struggles of people in Moss Side and Hulme. He shows the power of institutional and public images of the community; local people have to understand and resist this stereotyping, and doing this can sap their energy, turn their attention away from children's concerns and priorities. The author's interests in the American 'Rites of Passage' programmes springs partly from the programmes' base of theoretical ideas. This helps to bring the focus back from the 'macro' problems facing the area to the lives of children and young people and to the scope for developing positive images.

The chapter by Roger Adams draws on personal and professional experiences to give a perspective on children and communities which argues for greater recognition of place in children's lives. He illustrates the potential of his theme with an example from a community project, and he draws on environmental psychology literature. The chapter highlights the question of who, when children cannot speak for themselves, will advocate on their behalf.

The final chapter in this part presents the adult–child dilemmas referred to above. Building on previous work (Hasler, 1988), the author explores the meaning of community in terms of a shared experience and common humanity. He underlines the importance of the neighbourhood for children. In this way the chapter makes explicit a hidden tension running through many of the chapters between the discussion of children and neighbourhoods, and that of children and empowerment. They are not the same.

This part of the book is permeated by examples of practice. Through them, the case for paying attention to the intangible aspects of neighbourhood life, to co-operation between people, is restated. This is not a fashionable perspective to put forward. It does not sit easily with the functional, objective-setting character of contemporary regeneration programmes. The strong message of the three chapters, however, is that policy makers and managers will have to engage with the complexities of neighbourhood and community if programmes are to be meaningful to the lives of children and adults.

References

Etzioni, A. (1993) *The Spirit of Community*, New York: Crown Publishers.

Hasler, J. (1988) 'Community Development – Is it Child Care?' in *Working with Communities*, ed. P. Henderson, London: The Children's Society.

8 The Fear of Our Own Children

Craig Russell

Three young boys, two with bandannas over their faces, were running along the walkway, passing boarded-up flats, ducking into stairwells and calling to one another to watch out to the left, then beware the doorway to the right. The pieces of wood in their hands were being levelled and pointed at imaginary figures all around them.

Playground talk in some local primary schools was about the violence and the drug-based posses of that particular neighbourhood. The question was, which posse are you a member of – the Doddington, the Pepperhill mob or the Gooch?

For children to explore their environment, discover how to relate to the people around them, find a role for themselves, the imagination is a powerful resource. If the images that shape that mental world are guns, gangs, fast cars and death, it is easy to trace how they take a hold of a child's thinking. When those images surround you from the television, the computer game, your family's friend's and neighbour's talk, and when these pictures contrast so markedly with the dull grey environment of where you live, it is plain to see how and why they are brought to life in a child's mind and in children's play.

This chapter attempts to grapple with these realities and images as faced by the children, parents, teachers, community workers and youth leaders in the communities of Moss Side and Hulme in Manchester. I start with a narrative to recall the shooting of Benji Stanley, a terrible story that created the picture of this particular community for millions of people as it was flashed across the papers and television screens in this country, Europe and North America in January 1993. The story will open up several of the key factors that need to be borne in mind in relation to the wider issues of community development in an area such as Hulme and Moss Side.

The main argument of the chapter is that children, especially black children, carry the greatest burden for the economic collapse of our inner cities. The analysis will be set in the context of the 'underclass' debate, to see how selective images have created the rhetoric to be used to set political agendas. The role of the media is of vital importance, especially the way the debate can be manipulated to divert discussion from the underlying causes of the economic marginality and social collapse of many outer-estate and inner-city areas of Britain. What community development insights have emerged to assist those working with children, where social and economic exclusion, disaffection and violence are dominant features in the community where the child is to grow up?

On 3 January 1993 John 'Benji' Stanley, aged 14, was shot dead with a single-barrelled shotgun while waiting for dumplings in Alvino's, a take-away 100 yards from his home. The *Guardian* of the following day relied on a local boy of seven to tell the story:

> 'We can tell you what happened, Mister. The man had a punch gun, the kind you go choom-choom with,' said the little boy, indicating a pump action.
>
> 'He had a gun like Terminator's. I knew he wasn't from around here for everyone has automatic guns. He ran out and got into a car that had its doors open. There was music blasting out of it.' He and his sister had been a block away from Alvino's on a mission to buy toffees, when they heard the first shots going off.

Benji Stanley was the innocent victim of murder, but his death was not an isolated incident, it was the most recent in a series of shootings in inner-city Manchester. There is still nothing to link his death directly with the drugs and firearms rackets, but it has taken place in Moss Side which has been labelled 'Gunchester', 'Baby Beirut' and 'Britain's Bronx' by the serious press as well as the tabloids. In the previous 12 months six other people had been murdered in this area of one and half square miles, and at that time shootings were occurring on at least a weekly basis. To set Benji's death in the context of other drug-related crime is part of the story, but this alone gives no understanding of why this situation arose. Neither does it give any indication of appropriate responses for community development strategies for work with children.

For many years local teachers, parents and community leaders have warned of the serious nature of the violence amongst young people: 'the rains were seen coming but no one was prepared to help build an ark'. The escalation in the number of shootings over the last five years can be related to the changes in three factors: policing methods; drug availability and the culture of the rackets; and the wider economic decline.

Policing

In understanding the alienation of young people, policing in the area has been identified as a key concern for at least 20 years. In this location workers and researchers in the early 1970s warned of what might result from what was seen as the harassment of young people, the regular pattern of being picked up, questioned and then released without being charged. This was not taken very seriously by many in positions of leadership at that time, but from the point of view of those who were picked up and the understanding from hindsight now, it resulted in a feeling of racial victimisation, and a deep distrust of the police's intentions. The breakdown at this stage, caused through misunderstanding and direct racial and class prejudice, has a direct relationship with the frustrations, lack of trust and hostility experienced today.

When it came to the mid 1980s the police were openly talking about parts of Moss Side and Hulme being not just unpoliceable but as no-go areas after certain times. Comments by individual officers, who stated the area was 'no go', may have been flippant but to many local people this seemed the practice. The perception of the police's policy for the area was one of containment, keeping problems in a limited area and waiting for the appropriate time to pick off the main criminals. Genuine communication between the police and even community leaders was minimal and any trust virtually non-existent.

Drugs

During the late 1980s there was an increasing awareness that guns were coming into use by a few members of the community who were following the money that could be made out of drugs and increased competition in this market. As a consequence, police intervention in the area became more targeted and deliberately publicised across the rest of the city. Small-scale early morning police raids had been an established part of police operations, but in the early 1990s the scale of police action increased to orchestrated raids on dozens of houses in limited areas during the early morning.

In August 1991 Operation China resulted in 22 drug dealers being gaoled for a total of 90 years. In July 1992 a similar 6 a.m. raid was carried out, but this time television cameras were there to film the police action. The fact that the film crews were there must have made the task of making arrests more difficult, but this factor was overridden by the local political needs of the police to be seen by the general public to be acting decisively and successfully in this area. The filming of such actions would also need political sanction: to broadcast early-morning raids on parts of the black community for drugs and firearms, in an area of intense national and local economic and political intervention, could serve the agendas of various politicians of council and government.

These operations were hailed as a great success by the police. With many of the senior drug dealers in prison, gaps were left in the supply side of the market for their 'lieutenants' to fill. The spate of violence that occurred in the early 1990s was due to the next generation of dealers fighting it out over who would control the different areas for selling. Children, being on the street, seeing what was going on, exploring and checking things out, were drawn into these dynamics. They were used as messengers, deliverers, lookouts, and through this they gained their own 'respect' and found their own positions within groups.

The main trade in drugs up to the mid 1980s had been around marijuana. This had been very openly sold on popular street corners, from particular shops and in the central shopping area. Most of the people involved in this trade did not move into the 'heavier' drugs when these became the main focus of the market. But the people who did soon realised the financial potential of this business. Individual incomes of £1,000 a week were been talked about from around 1987. The Manchester drugs industry was supposedly turning over £20 million a year in the early 1990s. BMWs and Mercedes, expensive mountain bikes, mobile phones and top-of-the-range-clothes were and are the symbols of success in the drugs trade as in other lines of business.

Economic Decline

Throughout the 1980s, alongside this growing part of the economy, the vast majority of children and young people in the area saw their parents in worsening relative poverty, with less security and given less respect. Most people in the area who were in work were employed in low-paid jobs: domiciliary work in local hospitals, the construction industry, packing and warehouse work or with the council. As those children grew up their job prospects were minimal, and for the majority the only option was a 'scheme'. A few local clergymen were proud of the fact that they 'employed', second only to the council, the highest numbers of local people; this was through community programme and then employment training schemes. Since the 1981 uprisings, Moss Side and Hulme had been full of low-pay or no-pay training schemes, specially targeted to help create a labour force of the young people. A very small number of those people went on to other forms of employment.

The next experiment to tackle inner-city economic collapse was government intervention to inject the enterprise culture. The national Task Force initiatives of 1987 were able to offer small pots of money and business advice for those who were willing to 'go it alone' and set up commercial enterprises. With the amount of money available in the communities and in Task Force coffers, the number of legitimate enterprises that could be set up and survive was severely restricted. Realising that the social and economic situation in these communities was getting much worse, and that the interventions throughout the 1980s were hardly touching the increasingly desperate conditions, plans were made by central government, with collaboration from the local authority, to attempt, as far as possible, to wipe the area clean and start again.

Hulme and some parts of Moss Side were again in the midst of large-scale demolition and rebuilding programmes. This has come about from major government capital injections through City Challenge, the Housing Corporation and other channels, totalling in the region of £50 million, with corporate financing bringing in at least another £50 million. However, there are serious questions as to whether the way in which this capital is being used is for the benefit of existing residents and their future generations. The finance is primarily for building work and is put in the hands of large development companies. As it washes in and out of the area the only way for local people to get hold of it is through local labour schemes. These schemes account for up to 33 per cent of the labour force employed in the construction of the new Hulme and the parts of Moss Side being redeveloped. While this percentage of local people employed in the reconstruction of the area may be relatively high, the percentage of the amount of money that will be held in the community by them is miniscule next to the total capital involved.

These redevelopment programmes are a direct result of the social and economic problems of the local population, but by looking deeper it is seen that it is not the priorities of the local population that shape the targeting of the money. The redevelopment is primarily to regenerate the area socially and economically through restructuring the population and removing the unregenerated 'problems' (Massey and Denton, 1993).

The real political power remains in the hands of developers and financiers, so resources are focused on housing and environmental works. The process has exacerbated the social and economic needs of many local people by disrupting or destroying community networks, and could well result in simply moving the very same identified 'problems' into other parts of the city. To address social and economic needs requires a far more sophisticated and committed long-term approach than the current redevelopment of the area is permitting.

A concern for children growing up in the area was an important stimulation to each of the initiatives mentioned above. Local churches responded to the 1981 youth uprising by using the Manpower Services Commission and training and work schemes. The local Task Force was primarily targeted at unemployed black young people. The housing redevelopment work in Moss Side aims to open up cul-de-sacs, making estates more penetrable by police, keeping young drug dealers off the streets. There are numerous analyses of Hulme's problems, and why major redevelopment was called for. An essential point, in relation to our theme, is that the many millions of pounds for redevelopment would not have been drawn on if the system-built housing had been appropriate to house families which included young children.

Many millions of pounds have been and are being spent on these initiatives, but how do they measure up to the needs of local children and young people? Despite, and maybe in some ways because of, the Community Programme, Employment Training and the Task Force, the stark reality remains that over 80 per cent of black young men and in the region of 30 per cent of young, black women in the area are unemployed. Despite the availability of over £100 million to be spent in Hulme, after redevelopment the community will have lost a secondary school and well over 1,000 homes for low-income families. The number of homeless households in Manchester will be increased through the demolition of council accommodation in Hulme and the turning over of the land to private developers. Because of the way redevelopment has been implemented in many parts of the estate, resulting in major dislocations of family and friendship networks, there has been a rocketing of serious juvenile crime.

The three interwoven factors of drugs, unemployment and policing in this text need to be understood in their own terms, but there is also a need to see how they hold one another in place. A strategy addressing just one factor will not be successful, it will soon be undermined as a result of negative or no action in another. The drug rackets and related violence soon cause incoming industry and commerce to have cold feet. To arrest dealers without creating good employment opportunities for succeeding generations simply introduces new young people to the drugs market. Heavy and prejudiced policing helps enforce any sense of alienation from broader society among young people, and reinforces the disaffection of groups. As all three factors feed on one another the effect soon becomes a downward spiral. This spiral not only has a momentum of its own, it also creates a vortex into which other aspects of the community's life are sucked – hence the hold that the culture of drugs and violence can have over the thinking and behaviour of even the youngest children.

Having seen the results of many of these government interventions in inner-city communities, it would be naive to believe the idea that genuine concern for children growing up in Hulme and Moss Side was a major motivating factor – rather the motive is a *fear* of the children of these areas, and what they may become. Riots, drugs, uncontrollable young men are images used to trigger a reaction and resources, but each image creates a pathology that readily blames the victim, and which then shapes the intervention for the whole community. If we are looking for appropriate community development strategies for work with children in economically marginalised communities, it is crucial to see how the images created for different communities shape the forms of government intervention. This is seen in the way in which the media, ministerial rhetoric and government legislation relate to the term 'the underclass'.

The Media and the 'Underclass'

The concept of the 'underclass' in this discussion is important in that it forms the underlying framework for much of the media coverage of areas such as Hulme and Moss Side. The coming of phrases such as 'Baby Beirut', 'Britain's Bronx' or 'Gunchester' which are then repeated throughout all sections of the press and media, gives some indication of how the process of labelling occurs. How does the media condense what is a very complicated set of economic and social circumstances into a story? Commercial and political dictates have to ensure that an 'outside' viewer will be able to relate to the story immediately, usually in a way that will be non-threatening to expectations, established stereotypes or media language. The 'truth' of a story, in the ever more commercialised media, is in the interest and excitement that it can generate to attract the public and thus sponsors.

A spate of full page or colour supplement articles about Hulme and Moss Side were run in the serious press through January and February 1993, and were then mirrored in television documentaries. All had the same attributes. Night shots, the wheels of fast cars, the young black men, figures silhouetted against a light or wearing a mask, all became totems for the media as they attempted to relay what they thought the general public wanted to know about the area. Through this experience it became evident to local people that the news coverage and the feature articles had far more to do with what was in the mind of the journalist and the viewer than with what was really happening within their communities at large.

As newspaper editors chose headings and slogans to introduce the story of Benji Stanley's murder, each resorted to sensationalism: 'Gun law is running Manchester at the moment', 'Forget the police. They're nonentities', 'Climate of fear' (*Observer*); 'Is the death of Benji Stanley a sign that Britain is set on a course of ghetto violence to match the worst excesses of America? The *Mail* sent a distinguished American journalist to investigate' (*Daily Mail*); 'Killing marks new dimension in "Gunchester" Violence' (*Guardian*); 'Gun culture runs murder estate', 'If only he'd lived somewhere else' (*Independent*); 'Stay in or die', 'Benji, 14 murdered by mistake in ghetto where guns are just a fashion accessory' (*Daily Mirror*).

The resulting effect of this newspaper coverage on attitudes locally and on the general public can be seen to be two-fold: it has enhanced the profile, the prestige and ultimately the power of the serious drug dealer in the community; and it has enlarged the divide between these particular neighbourhoods and the rest of society. Little if any light has been shed to help people understand what these communities are like or the reasons behind the desperation and violence that are undeniably a part of their experience. A cynic may say that all the mainstream media are deliberately blowing up the images and creating stereotypes of these communities in order to sell papers. A more liberal position may still hold to the argument that the 'truth' has to be portrayed even if it then falls into the hands of those who may use it against the 'victims'. There is a story that a *Guardian* journalist went to Moss Side to get a story about the positive elements about the community, only to be told on his return to the paper that this was not the image the *Guardian* wanted to portray about the area. The critique that the press is more about opinion forming than investigation takes some refuting, and as the liberal press starts to use an underlying analysis shaped by an understanding that an underclass exists, it is important to ask what opinions it is hoping to form.

An examination of the construct of the underclass is important because it sets the experience of Hulme and Moss Side in the wider context in two ways. It shows how particular aspects of that community's life, notably violence and drugs, can be seized upon and used out of all proportion to set a political and economic agenda for an area. Secondly, the analysis can open up lessons from this particular community which can be compared with and applied to settings in Europe and North America. While the experiences of Hulme and Moss Side do have particular dimensions, an added level of exclusion is created because of racism, there are many parallels to be drawn with marginal white working-class communities throughout Britain and the west, many of whom have also suffered riots, drugs, violence and economic disregard, inappropriate policing and manipulative media.

For those who are economically, politically, and socially excluded there is nothing to be gained at this point in history from accepting the term 'underclass'. It has little if any potential for creating cohesion in broad-based movements, and is more likely to elicit sympathy and fear rather than solidarity among potential supporters. The term is a tool that is being used to manipulate both political and intellectual debate and popular perceptions. 'Underclass' is being loosely used in this country to group together divergent people such as single mothers, squatters, black people, long-term unemployed people, irresponsible fathers, homeless people, travellers, young people without jobs, people living in so-called 'sink estates'. Definitions of the term deliberately revolve around any supposed negative 'attributes' of people in the group, which are then labelled together as dysfunctional. Its systematic usage is designed to build up the blame on the 'victim', ignoring the situation of inequality of opportunity, relative poverty or oppression and consumerist exploitation. This 'negative labelling' adds another barrier between those already excluded and their full economic and political participation in society. We need to understand a more precise definition of the terms and the context in which it was coined. Alongside that it will be useful to examine alternative analyses and strategies for facing the phenomenon of exclusion and alienation.

Rites of Passage Programmes

The term underclass is derived from the United States, and it is to there that many have looked to seek an appropriate way of facing up to the construct. Among the most powerful of the responses, and the approaches that hold the most integrity in relation to the principles of community development, are those under the broad heading of the 'Rites of Passage' programmes. These have proved an inspiration to a number of the activists, workers and projects in the Hulme and Moss Side area. The approach has been pioneered and developed by black theoreticians and activists in the United States, but its application may well be transferable to black British experience, and it may possibly be valuable to explore how some of the principles could be applied to marginalised white working-class communities as well.

The main theoretical ideas to be explored here have been developed by the poet and theoretician E.U. Perkins. In one of his earliest books, *Home is a Dirty Street: The Social Oppression of the Black Child*, Perkins describes the plight of black children and youths in the United States by looking at the disproportionate numbers of black young people who are locked in the juvenile justice system, hooked on drugs and alcohol, disenchanted with school, alienated from their parents, and disenfranchised from legitimate opportunities to gain meaningful employment. He contrasts this with the experience of the 'bumpies', the increasing numbers of black graduates whom he sees as focusing on themselves as individuals and adopting values supposedly void of any racial references, and clearly shaped by the dominant culture. He highlights the increasing numbers of black young people who suffer mental illness or who have seen murder or have committed suicide. He also goes part of the way with those developing the underclass analysis by noting the escalation of black young people with teenage pregnancies, and what he calls the 'high risks associated with single parent families' leaving many with 'questionable futures'. He identifies many of these problems as being caused by a system of oppression that creates the 'ghetcolony' – a term used to describe the so-called black ghetto.

To survive in this system, black young people find refuge in the 'street institution', where they learn to live under prescribed norms and values taught by adults whose lifestyles are often self-defeating. However, the street institution acts as an oppressive harness that takes its toll on each new generation. Ultimately he sees this form of socialisation as being defined and controlled by white America.

In the book *Harvesting New Generations: The Positive Development of Black Youth*, Perkins moves on from this description of the desperate situation of many black young people to re-express and develop the ideas of 'rites of passage'. He draws from the idea of 'Poro' in Alex Haley's book *Roots*, where Kunta Kente is indoctrinated with the spiritual and cultural manifestations of his people's traditions that consummate his manhood. Through this Perkins explores African traditions of childhood and pre-adolescent experiences, how they were arranged in an orderly fashion enabling young people to adapt to the values and morals of their society, and creating a highly disciplined and respectful attitude towards family and elders. He examines how these traditions were broken down and deliberately suppressed through the experience of slavery, destroying even the most fundamental roles of parenthood. From here he looks at the evolution of culture, its gradual formation and easy destruction, and the stages of the 'socialisation environment' of black young people from their African roots to the present US experience.

In moving to the present day he picks up the term 'underclass', as it was being used in the US in the early 1980s. From a *Time Magazine* cover story of 1982, he quotes:

> The barricades are seen only fleetingly by most middle class
> Americans as they rush by in their cars or commuter trains

. . . but out there is a different world, a place of pockmarked streets, gutted tenements and broken hopes . . . behind its crumbling walls lives a large group of people who are more intractable, more socially alien and more hostile than almost anything imagined. They are the unreachables: the American Underclass.

This extract has many resonances with media coverage of Moss Side and Hulme, and some British journalists have clearly lifted their style of journalism and basic analysis from the US. Perkins points to the research of American academic Douglas G. Glasgow (1987) which highlights the time lag between the social reality experienced by black people in the 1960s and the media that picked up the phrase 'the underclass' 20 years later. The impact of that analysis is now hitting our press another ten years on.

Some of the analysis of the underclass is accepted by Perkins, but its conclusion – blaming the victim – he will not swallow. The victim as scapegoat is the inevitable political solution for those on the right. What Perkins seeks to do is express the same experience in terms of oppression and exploitation. From within that he looks for the positive aspects of the cultural heritage, including those that have been long suppressed, to find a way of making sense of history consistent with an African identity, personality and philosophical foundation. One formulation of this ethos is based on collective consciousness and focused on positive forms of relationship: 'I am because we are and because we are, therefore, I am.' This is then elaborated into a set of behavioural modes in Afro-American children. What he is attempting to do is to move on from the stages of 'black consciousness' of the 1960s and 'Afro-centrism' of the 1970s to analyse how these can be interpreted and codified in relation to contemporary African-American experience. This systemised code will later form the basis for the educational programme 'rites of passage'.

Throughout his analysis Perkins has intimated the sort of practical approaches that should be taken to counteract the disabling aspects of the dominant culture of the US, as well as developing a powerful critique of that socio-political system. Towards the end of his book he draws this together in an outline conceptual model for the positive development of black youth.

To put a rites of passage programme into practice he outlines the structures of a social group organised with a community of elders who have the responsibility for helping to train young people to become responsible adults, accepting that young people cannot sufficiently teach themselves to become adults, and that their social-isation of young people must be channelled through institutions that provide them with critical guidance and support systems. These structures are to offer a programme that clearly challenges the codes and values of the broader society and that takes as central the concept of Afro-centricity.

British Context

There is a history and particular social context out of which the rites of passage programmes have grown but from which many parallels can be drawn within the Afro-Caribbean communities of Britain. The deepest roots are clearly the same: the experience of slavery, cultural displacement and economic oppression. There are clear differences of histories of black struggle against slavery in each of the Caribbean islands and also in the US, but similar-ities can be seen. The similarities of contemporary experiences of the US and Britain are also becoming better understood. The hopes and expectations of black people from the Caribbean of the 1950s migration have turned to a large extent to disillusion, and are now more clearly understood in terms of racism, economic exploitation, unemployment and minority status. This mirrors the experience of the 'ghetcolonies' on the other side of the Atlantic.

In Moss Side and Hulme a great deal of work has been carried out around African/black culture and roots. This has grown indige-nously within the community, but has also drawn on African-American experience and direct from historical and con-temporary Africa. Most of the work has been in the fields of culture and education. The Abasindi Centre in Moss Side has proved to be a key focus for clarifying and developing identity both for individuals and also a wide part of the community, especially for local women. The centre's cultural programme in the 1980s developed around African dance, music and art. The work tapped and adapted vital understandings and forms from across Africa.

Alongside this ran educational work, primarily with children, that picked up on threads from within the African cultural heritage. Several people who, ten years on, are key activists in the community, or who have been through great personal pain and loss in part due to racism, were children when this programme was running. They still point to it as the most important element of their formation; they would say that it has motivated and sustained them through their most challenging experiences. Abasindi as a centre was closed down due to the poor state of the building and lack of funds in 1992. Some of the people involved went on to form the Abasindi Women's Dance Group, which has had wide recognition nationally and internationally. The focus for black cultural work has now moved to the NIA Centre in Hulme. This is more commercially oriented, and provides a platform for black musicians from across the world.

The work with children in schools is another key area where foundations have been laid to engage with the challenges this community faces. Several black people who had been schooled in Hulme and Moss Side and had seen how the educational system had failed a disproportionate number of their black friends decided to become teachers themselves. Throughout their formal sessions at teacher training college they found very little that directly addressed the particular needs of black people, so they started to develop their own resources with which to teach black pupils. A great deal of their material was derived from the US and its major focus was on black culture, history and literature. As they have gone on in their careers, they have gathered African educational material to be applied to religion, maths and physical education as well as many other parts of the school syllabus. The pioneering work of building up a black educational programme was not viewed favourably because of the perceived threat to the established syllabus.

As soon as the creative potential of ideas derived from the rites of passage programmes are put into practice within the existing formal school setting the problems become self-evident if not overwhelming. To support and broaden out this 'movement' a national conference was held in April 1993 on the theme of education of the black child. The main input was from African Americans and its appeal was well beyond the expectations of the organisers, with around 400 people attending the weekend from across the country.

Concluding Comments

As outlined at the start of this chapter, among the greatest obstacles to the development of the communities of Hulme and Moss Side is the drug culture and the violence connected with it. Children are possibly closer to this than any other innocent parties within the community. They are probably more likely to find used syringes, most often out of doors, than other groups in the community, and they are more likely than their parents to be told by older siblings what is happening on the street. Their closeness to the inevitable tragedies is shown in the story of the shooting of Benji Stanley. Children's closeness to such horrific incidents cannot be ignored. Children's involvement within the community action subsequent to Benji's death was very important. It helped them work through what was happening, and brought home to the community and the general public the deeper issues of child development and creation of community in such an area.

The Moss Side and Hulme Community Forum, that draws together many local people, organised a march through the area soon after Benji's funeral. Placards linking the drugs trade to lack of job options and the withdrawal of resources from the inner city were carried, and alongside these there was a very high percentage of children carrying placards with the simple, personally drawn messages 'No to Drugs' and 'No to Violence'. Their presence in such action in their own community was an extremely powerful sight. During the speeches at the end of the march a poem was read that had been written by a 13-year-old local girl:

> When I heard the news of Benji,
> It brought a tear to my eye.
> Another murder in the Moss,
> I can't say that I was surprised.
>
> Children of today
> Are the children of tomorrow.
> We don't need anymore tragedies
> To express our sorrow.
>
> We don't need any more examples
> Of how easy it is to die.
> We don't need to see wailing fathers
> Or see our parents cry.
>
> Shooting, fighting,
> Drugs, backbiting.
> This is the news we don't want highlighting.
> What we need is strength and unity,
> Not this violence in my community.

We are here we are gathered
It shows that we care
It shows that there is not violence everywhere
Marching and chanting
Our voices will be heard . . .

No more shooting!

No more killing!

No more violence!

No more drugs!

Moss Side belongs to us!

The approach that I have taken here has been to look at images, how they are created and used: child in bandanna, black person, drugs and violence, underclass. The approach has not denied the underlying questions of broader politics and economics that ultimately give shape to all that is happening in Hulme and Moss Side. The hope of the approach has been that through exploring and exploding the images created for this community we can more clearly see the motives and values of those that have most powerfully created the shape of human lives that are commonly presented from these communities. Through what the public are shown and the way resources are controlled, politicians and the media working hand in glove determine what this area is, and what it is to be. This does not deny any individual responsibility on the part of people involved in violence, and it is clear that the community and its leaders have responsibility for what happens. But their role and responsibility must be set alongside the determining power over resources and image manipulation which are held by others. It is the weakness and negative aspects of these communities that dominate public perceptions, and it is these that are then responded to by politicians. In that response it is the agenda of national government that becomes the determinant, into which the actual needs and local ideas are subsumed.

A critique of the economic and political situation alone is not sufficient if adults are going to help transform local situations. However, knowing of the experiences of children and marginalised communities, so often seemingly without the economic, social and political leverage to confront and transform the problems they face, where do adults turn to help develop community?

The communities of Moss Side and Hulme are battling to develop positive images of themselves and their own cultures. At the same time, they are maintaining a critique of the institutions which intervene to shape the area's future. The ideas clustered around 'rites of passage' focus on history, identity, belonging, respect and responsibility. Within this there is still a great deal to express in relation to the value base of 'rights of passage', its potential in helping to secure and develop identities, and how rites of passage programmes can be used as an organisational structure. The ideas of the Roots movement, of black people knowing and respecting who they are, is the foundation of the rites of passage. This is now being built on by working through the questions of social responsibility and organisation, how the individual is to act within the group, the community, and broader society.

The dangers are that the ideas and organisations discussed here could implode if developed along separatist or black nationalist lines. But if they are seen and used as a means of affirming self-respect and community responsibility for black people within multi-ethnic approaches the strength will be powerful, and the lessons applicable to other marginalised groups of different cultural backgrounds and identities.

Children are central to future programmes based on 'rites of passage'. I have shown the extent to which they have been drawn into the problems of Moss Side and Hulme; only by working with them on a basis of trust and mutual respect will adults gain their support and positive involvement. This takes us back to the themes explored by Paul Henderson in the Introduction to this book, and to his argument that policy makers should take the subject of children and community development more seriously. The addressing of crises within our inner-cities, and the formulating of redevelopment ideas must be based on a deep concern for our children's futures and not on a fear of them.

References

Glasgow, Douglas G. (1987) *The Black Underclass: Poverty, Unemployment and Entrapment of Ghetto Youth*, New York: Vintage Books.

Massey, Douglas S. and Denton, Nancy A. (1993) *American Apartheid: Segmentation and the Making of the Orderclass,* Harvard: Harvard University Press.

Perkins, Useni Eugene (1975) *Home is a Dirty Street: The Social Oppression of the Black Child,* Chicago: Third World Press.

Perkins, Useni Eugene (1985) *Harvesting New Generations: The Positive Development of Black Youth,* Chicago: Third World Press.

9 Places of Childhood

Roger Adams

Along with several colleagues I recently completed a recording of our memories of the neighbourhoods in which we spent our middle childhoods (7 to 14 years old). I found myself describing how important it was to me that there was 'a hill ridge somewhere to place my land of marvels' (W.H. Auden).

There was choice in my world: I could go to the Clay Banks, the waste land, the mysterious lost village of Gunthorpe; I could walk to see a girl on a farm a mile away in the next village; I could cycle the three miles into Oakham or take the bus to Stamford. Colin Ward (1988), exploring the theme of children and rurality, notes that England in the 1950s was when public transport was at its best.

At the end I was exploring the growth of my relationship with the outside world. My memory is of freedoms explored in a good place, for children belonging to a period when the word 'children' was not always in a bracket with problems. Children were not seen, in adult eyes, as harbingers of disorder.

The intuition gained from this learning lead me to the following propositions. First, a sense of place during childhood leads to a commitment to preserve the integrity of the communities known in adult life. Second, this place identity depends on the previous bonding of the child with the close natural world discovered during middle childhood. Just as we bond with parents in the early years so we bond with nature in middle childhood. Third, the link between place identity and bonding is play, given that children 'own' their play.

My intention is to examine how present-day neighbourhoods construct childhood. I do this in the hope that community work practitioners will develop a mission and reasoning for a practice that is child focused. It should be a part of their purpose to disturb stereotypes of childhood with an alternative perspective. I urge practitioners to put into perspective the state's worries about how functional are the socialising institutions of family and school and to find ways of including children's experiences in their work. What is happening at street level to enable children to value their lives in neighbourhoods?

In middle age the value of having once formed a place identity is not a minor sub-identity. It is because as a child I knew stress in my family and school and yet had the choice of intense joyful experience in my access to places of play in nature that today I know how to recuperate from the struggle to survive. That is why it is crucial to attend to place identity and the fostering of the relationship between the child and the natural world. Yet childhood exploration of self and place is being destroyed. While David Sobel (1990) has written that he has discovered forts in the backyards of New England, on the banks of Floridas Suwannee River and in the urban woodlands of Washington DC, children in many of Britain's urban communities are saying that their streets are so dangerous they cannot reach parks and other play areas (see Titman, 1994).

This chapter is written with the expectation that readers will recall the sources of themselves formed by association with place. The approach encourages internal dialogue and the making of meanings that only participation with children at street level will fully clarify.

The novelist John Fowles has written about how his father grew fruit trees at their suburban London home. He had a garden of close-packed fruit trees which he pruned heavily. Fowles saw in this the cut-down nature of his father's life. The social and economic impact of the First World War directed and controlled his life. By contrast Fowles recalls the time his family moved to Dorset during the Second World War as the occasion when he began to learn how to explore nature and how it represented to him a self of creativity, spirit and imagination:

> It is immaterial that I do not cultivate trees in any sense my father would recognise or credit. He would never have conceded that my thirty acres of scrub and pasture was my equivalent of his own beautifully disciplined apples and pears and just as much cultivated. His chaos happens to be my creative order. (Fowles, 1992, p. 26)

I believe that places of nature in children's lives give rise to a sense of attachment and meaning that will affect thoughts and feelings about self. The process of attachment can go on for years with a layering of successive play episodes. And the result of this intensity of experience of place will be reflected in a sense of being strong enough to use 'placeness' and rootedness to describe the feeling of affiliation.

The City Child

Hillman, Adams and Whitelegg (1990) make a connection between the internal spaces of the child and the loss to children of their neighbourhoods because of the actions of adults. They look to the future and wonder at the psychological cost to the child of the loss of independent movement over the last 20 years. They point to how responsibility is essential for the development of self-esteem. They underline the intensity of family relationships and the absence of the relief of going out to play. It is considered by some psychologists that television provides a substitute for physical space in that, at least mentally, it removes children from their immediate family environment and gives them a chance to enter another world.

What the authors say supports the environment and childhood. But within the last observation I see a useful point connecting and comparing present self-experience within a place with that of the past. I notice that yesterday's children writing in my local Colne (Lancashire) newspaper often want to tell the story of the history of their lives. What interests me is that they do this out of the images created of the places of their childhood. The richness of recall is actually the story of a childhood time in which the child freely explored the outside world. The value attaching to the experience is clear in the story told.

I cannot critically review neighbourhood and the child and not recognise how the control of adults over places of nature has arisen from a fear that children have become vandals in their neigh-bourhoods, and in return how children may view the adults as despoilers intent on making an anti-children environment. When children allow an adult into their lives on the streets what they reveal to the inquirer is an holistic self-experience, one in which their play links self and place. The pages of *Childhood Domain* by R.C. Moore (1986) are full of quotations reflecting his immersion in the phenomenology of childhood environments. They depict how close is the relationship between nature, child and family environment:

> This was no wasteland I began to realise, but a peaceful haven, moments from the cramped and dingy basement where Heather lived. The more Heather talked about this fertile land the more it began to acquire a rich new significance invisible to me moments before. There was a real sense of childhood possession there in a place temporarily abandoned by the adult world. Child, parents and physical environment seemed to form a close knit trinity . . .
>
> The poor micro-climate of Gill's play area was greatly exacerbated by the wind tunnel effect – caused by the tall buildings that had replaced the sheltering terraces formerly occupying the site. The place had none of the playful ambience of Heather's wasteland haven. The positive aspects of Heather's situation seemed completely absent in Gill's case. Living sixty or seventy feet above an unresponsive ill-defined playscape had helped to breed apprehension and ignorance instead of trust and understanding. (Moore, 1988, pp. 2 and 5)

All of the above will remain excluded knowledge until practitioners develop a perspective on childhood that links this knowledge to practice. There has to be a real intention to listen to children. Practitioners, particularly those based on neigbourhood centres such as that described in Chapter 1 above, have to explore with children in their localities the nature of their stories of local childhood.

A Children's Project

The Vauxhall inner London project of The Children's Society escaped the management by objective assumptions. By this I mean that the project was not founded with the assumption of technical problem-solving by choosing the best means suited to the achievement of intended objectives. Instead the project was a practical inquiry in which the children were not 'the planned for' but were in conversation with the practitioners, talking back to them about values. Thus the project developed as an inquiry that included in its process shared decision making with the children. It was given this freedom because it had its origins in the hypothesis of a 'child in the neighbourhood research' project that set forth an holistic perspective on childhood. Practice action was to be creative. It was framed in terms of processes that would uncover children's values and realities in their neighbourhood in order to engage local adults in change towards that reality. This approach guided the project brief:

> What is happening to children in communities which are under economic and social pressure? What is it that disadvantages children and how can organised services respond in a way which values children?

And this was the formulation of the proposition into which the project would, with the children, inquire: 'The experience of neighbourhood is being eroded as a result of adult behaviour and concerns.'

The project began with conventional research methods that were intended to explore the perceptions of the place of the child in the neighbourhood of Vauxhall. Observations from 112 children were mainly about the effects of dog ownership and control; the littering of streets; the upkeep of play spaces; and the provision of library and recreational facilities. The estate football pitch was too small and unusable – 'There is one but its very small and it's got glass everywhere.'

A repeated theme was poor control of dogs or the prevalence of litter: 'Cos there's litter all over the place, there's poo everywhere from dogs.' Or both of these are just part of the general mess. 'Dogs poo poo on the floor, and rubbish, and peoples toilet leaking.' Meanwhile the flowers get destroyed.

The question most difficult to answer was about favourite place. Several children could not answer. This caused the researcher to observe that it may be that favourite places are found more when the environment as a whole is valued. If children do not value their environment (or themselves) then perhaps it is less easy to identify a favourite place.

The project broke into a truly participative inquiry when it gave the children resources to tell their story. It became a project that had as its objective children being heard. It offered them a two-week dance, drama and music experience.

Day one started with 12 children being asked to write down their individual likes and dislikes in the neighbourhood. But by the end of two weeks the central theme had become one of place and how play shapes experiences of place differently for children compared with adults.

Three professionals were engaged for the project, one skilled in community dance, one in community music and one in drama. The children were introduced to musical, dance and dramatic skills which engaged and involved their playfulness. The drama project was an innovative way of doing research with children. The recording of the processes of the drama project over its two weeks through observation, note taking and video, created a text which showed up a range of themes touched upon from the point of view of children and young people.

The concentration, involvement and imagination portrayed in the video touched what was of real importance. Three months after the project finished it was discovered that the council had plans to redevelop Vauxhall Park, reducing the amount of play equipment and removing play space. Lunch breaks on the project had been spent using this same equipment.

The drama script was the creation of the children and was spontaneous and wholly imaginative, and it changed from performance to performance. There were also different versions for the same scene. I offer two small extracts:

> Narrator: Here is a story about children being heard. The story is set in Vauxhall Park. But this is a very special park that only children can see and play in. To grown-ups it looks like a waste-land, but if you look through the hole in the fence it is the best park in the world.

And at the end, when they get their park back, the children sing:

> I have a place where I go when I feel crowded
> I have a place when I am surrounded on every side
> The time is all my own
> I go to be alone
> I have a place of my own.
> (Corbishley, nd, p. 8)

In the conclusion to the research report is the comment that 'bonding with neighbourhood takes place only when play is owned by the children and has its own space'. This is a warning that if the formation of the identity of the child is to be influenced by the place where the child lives then play is not for colonisation by adults. Leave it with children and protect their right to be the main users of the neighbourhood.

The success of the project can be judged not only by the involvement of the children in the two-week summer project, but by the effect it had on adults involved in organising the project who took up the theme of the loss of play space.

They realised that the local council intended to use Urban Programme funds to 'landscape' the local park where the children had taken their lunch breaks during the two weeks of the project. This meant that play facilities would, to quote the local Unitary Development Plan, be 'rationalised'. The kickabout area would be grassed over, and some of the play equipment used by the 8- to 14-year-olds would be placed in the areas presently set aside for families and toddlers. To date some success has been achieved in reducing the impact of the proposed 'improvement' by retaining more play space.

Equally important, this experience of trying to ensure that council officers were open to the views of local residents, including the views of the children themselves, led to a further intervention in the Unitary Development Plan itself. A variety of 'formal representations' were made to change the emphasis within the plan and point out the neglect of the children's perspective on the planning and management of play spaces in the neighbourhood. One local person pointed to the loss of a sense of neighbourhood from the volume of traffic on the main roads which trisect Vauxhall: the planners 'have damaged children's sense of Vauxhall as a place and neighbourhood for them to grow up in and develop'. Another person talked of the importance of co-ordination between the different agencies controlling and managing open space (e.g. Lambeth planning, housing, education and amenity services) in order to develop a common policy on children's place in the neighbourhood.

These comments were made after discussion with a further group of adults involved in 'Vision for Vauxhall,' a local forum of voluntary groups, tenants and businesses interested in planning developments affecting the neighbourhood. The work of the children in producing the play was being echoed in the efforts of a widening range of adults alerted to the loss of neighbourhood in the lives of local children.

Adult agencies need to be bold and skilled enough to support projects similar to the one in Vauxhall I have described, not because such an approach is 'progressive' or innovative but because it takes seriously the connections between children's sense of neighbourhood, play and identity.

Psychology and Place Identity

The idea of using the physical environment as a strategy for maintaining oneself is clearly accepted in psychological literature. Kimberly Davey (1990) concludes that although children are largely stuck with their inheritance, places of peace – of escape – and dreaming of sanity and imaginative independence can provide important opportunities that enable these children to endure with their sanity and imagination intact. I wonder if thought is seriously given to the child's need to escape from the violence and oppression which can leave a child scarred for life. I do not mean by escape holidays but a place in which to recuperate and which will support a place identity.

Michael Rutter (1979) has argued that children can readily adapt to a single major negative experience but are overwhelmed by multiple experiences of poverty and illness. No child can cope when put under too much stress. Resilience demands there be a balance between stressful life events and protective factors in the child's environment. Can we not see that each riot on an estate that tells of the breakdown of local social relationships that support children is the story also of the ending of hope, of a place of recuperation from emotional despair?

These are the voices of children interviewed about their fears and hopes of life on a Newcastle estate: 'People to be kind and stop picking children up'; 'Give more love an that'; 'Make the world nice instead of horrible and make the people next door to me nicer' (Wallace, in *Social Work Today*, 16 January 1992). The interviewers found that all the younger children mentioned the importance of the local park and that the common voice was that of wanting to leave the estate.

I think these voices utter, but then leave, the question about hope of a positive place identity. What hope is there of using the physical environment as a means of maintaining the psychic balance of pain and pleasure and the coherence of one's self and self-esteem, the hope of a favourite place of control and its humanising by the fixing of memories on it, there to find oneself?

The child most at risk of economic poverty and family fracture is the child most likely to live in a stressful neighbourhood where there is a hostile social environment. The stresses which affect children collect in neighbourhoods: poverty, racial conflict, crime, turbulent broken families, dogs, traffic and pollution merge with problems of acute stress such as illness, death and unemployment. All erode the networks and sources of support that sustain the emotional growth of children.

Sometimes the practitioner does not value what he or she is learning about children's lives at street level. I recall visiting a street on a north west council estate and one particular family on the street. With some of the perceptions from when I had been a psychiatric social worker, now I was visiting in the company of a community worker. The point of the visit for the worker was for the mother to relate what she had done in a project. I heard from the mother how families in the street were terrorised by the large dogs of other families. The fences between the back yards of the houses had all come down and the dogs had control. Most young children and lone mothers stayed in the safety of the houses sharing the same entrapped, anxiety-ridden world. The mother with other local people, having approached the community worker on the subject, formed an action group about the fences and eventually the fences were restored by the council. For the mother, her children had gained outside play spaces.

Whilst I heard this account of the mother gaining confidence through community life I was also hearing from her of her daughter's previous school refusal and of the 11-year-old daughter's once friendless lonely life which had mirrored that of her mother in their house-prison. I felt there was a probable psychological connection between the changes that had happened. The mother had the confidence to go to the action group and the daughter found a group of friends at the centre, there to begin a new self-experience. I saw that the mother, once away from imprisonment in her own home, could communicate to her daughter the message of neighbourhood as place, choice and opportunity, and for her daughter to follow her.

Korpela (1989), an environmental psychologist writing about place identity, provides inspiration in formulating the child/place proposition that I advocate. He shows how the act of encounter is one of actively using the physical environment in creating and maintaining the self. He holds that self-involvement in the physical environment is possible. What the child gains is an opportunity for the reflective moment in which to organise his or her feelings to find a recuperative place. The child therefore gains from place identity out of place belongingness. The functions of the self are enhanced because the time of reflection and the experience of being maintain self-coherence.

In my proposition the self is a story teller aiming at a high level of self-esteem which is obtained by having a coherent story. The place of childhood is where our environmental narrative begins. It is my belief that if community workers come to own this psychology in a different key, one which draws on environmental psychology and gives a voice to the child's experiences of place identity, they will speak for a childhood that does not bracket them with social work or formal education. Indeed they may well have a knowledge of childhood that is not understood by child welfare professionals who run child care services designed around an 'in-care' experience of childhood.

I recently heard of a child of nine referred to a project who, on being interviewed in court, could not say where she had come from. She had moved house eight times in her short life. I wonder what this means in mental health terms? One answer must be the capacity to cope with a high-risk environment. My hypothesis is that this child will not have a choice of belonging to place in a way which would sustain her existence as a person, and I predict that she will have no narrative of dwelling in a childhood place. I foresee that instead she may well rattle round the welfare system as a child in whom change has been promoted and measured by adults.

Who will speak for this child? Who understands her as a child disabled by the loss of her story of self and place? Each professional observer will only record her life in their system. Each record will compartmentalise her living by organisational responsibility. There will be a record of how those inside organisations see a child's life. Their records construct their meanings for her life. For place identity the school will have her address and will record her classroom behaviour. The social worker will have her home address on file to say how and where she is accommodated and with whom. None is a record of her accomplishing a growing place identity. None is in her voice, her own narrative of knowing self and place, by which she will tell her story of where she grew up.

But who *can* speak for her? When children leave the school gates organisations assume they belong to family life. Yet children do not have rights to take part in community life. No reference or value is given to the quality of the child's life on the streets. In some areas there may be some provision to bridge between family and school with additional adult supervision in the shape of after-school clubs, and in the holidays summer play schemes. Yet the provision is often an extension of organisational order in children's lives, not a policy recognition of children's ways of seeing how lives are constructed away from adults. The latter need constantly to remind themselves that children move between different 'systems' – home and family (or welfare), school and community. It is the third of these which is neglected by policy makers, and about which we need to learn more. If children do not have opportunities for play outside the adult domain, their sense of identity will be more difficult to establish, self-esteem harder to build up, and social adjustment – finding out how to live in and belong to a wider society – less likely to occur.

During the Second World War, and until 1953, there existed in Bermondsey, East London, the Children's Flats. They were places for children to have their own territory for play, experience and expression. The adults had a role of influence not authority. The flats ceased to function because the local authority could not categorise them within either welfare or education, and this remains a challenge for many local authorities.

I would like to see more local authorities follow the lead of Rochdale. There is a children's officer there who has a staff team of neighbourhood children's officers, and there is a children's committee which is concerned that there should be representation of children's interests within all of the local authority's departments. The children's officer asserts that:

> the structures are new, the results as yet relatively untested, but we feel that we have taken an important step forward, the major point of recognition being that we should be working towards a better service for the whole child. (Williams, 1992)

It is this kind of vision that is needed in order for the links between children and places in neighbourhoods to be rediscovered. If adults recall the importance of places in their own development they will be more willing to listen to what children say about their neighbourhoods and more prepared to encourage children-led activities. That is the challenge we face.

References

Corbishley, P. (nd) *A Parish Listens to Children*, London: The Children's Society.

Davey, K. (1990) 'Refuges and Imagination: Places of Peace in Childhood', *Children's Environments Quarterly*, vol. 6, no. 4.

Fowles, J. (1992) *The Tree*, St Albans: The Sumach Press.

Hillman, M., Adams, J., Whitelegg, J. (1990) *One False Move: . . . A Study of Children's Independent Mobility*, London: PSI.

Korpela, K.M. (1989) Place Identity as a Product of Environmental Self Regulation in *Journal of Environmental Psychology*, March.

Moore, R. (1986) *Childhood Domain: Play and Peace in Child Development*, London: Croom Helm.

Rutter, M. (1979) 'Protective Factors in Children's Responses to Stress and Disadvantage', M.W. Kent and J.E. Rolf eds. *Primary Prevention* of *Psychopathology*, vol. 3, Social Competence in Children (pp. 49–74) University of Pres, New England.

Sobel, D. (1990) 'A Place in the World: Adults' Memories of Childhoods' Special Places' in *Children's Environment Quarterly*, vol. 7, no. 4.

Titman, W. (1994) *Special Places; Special People*, London: World Wide Fund for Nature and Learning Through Landscapes.

Ward, C. (1988) *The Child in the Country*, London: Bedford Square Press.

Williams, R. (1992) *'The Impact of Children Today within a Metropolitan Borough'* (unpublished paper) Rochdale Metropolitan Borough Council.

Wallace, B. (1992) 'Living on the Edge' in *Social Work Today*, 16 January.

10 Belonging and Becoming – The Child Growing Up in Community

Joe Hasler

The question running through this chapter is, 'To what extent will the development of the 'child's right to choose' provide a useful principle in community development practice?' To approach this question I will consider the ways in which community projects engage with children and will then examine the nature of the child growing up in the community – or perhaps I should say the child's community. In social work terms, talk of 'the child growing up in the community' has come to mean growing up in the family setting, as opposed to being placed in a residential home, with little consideration of the community in which the family is set, other than perhaps the school.

First I hope to reflect on my experience of working on council housing estates in different parts of the country and to examine what it means to be a child growing up in these communities. Second, I will consider what kinds of connection community work projects make with the life of the child. What community work should we choose to do if we want to engage with the life of the child? Finally, I will raise the concept of children's rights and the extent to which it has a bearing upon neighbourhood-based community work.

Community Work Projects and Children

Community work projects set out to make a difference in a neighbourhood and engage with the people who live there on a whole range of issues. I have noticed three different approaches used by community work projects to the benefit of children and young people:

- face-to-face community work with children and young people
- community work with local adults to the benefit of their own and other people's children
- community work which is inter-generational and from which children benefit.

Some projects set out to make contacts with young people and children, and to offer them help in organising and planning a response to their own situation. A common example is of children and young people who have nowhere to meet. I remember a distraught mother coming to my door. Her son had been threatened by a gang of youths with bicycle chains at the bottom of the stairs to their block of flats. Gathering all the courage she could muster, she approached them and asked why they were hanging around in this particular place. They replied that they had nothing to do, and nowhere else to go where they could be together. Opposite her home was a community hall which seemed to provide for the elderly and several evenings of bingo. She pointed this out.

She had further conversations with the young people themselves, and with her husband and friends, and she came to believe that the young people could organise their own activities, but if the community hall was to be used then some adult presence would be required. The community worker was asked for help with the negotiations among the young people themselves, between them and the concerned adults, and between these parties and those who managed the community hall. There are many situations like this that involve community work with young people directly.

A community worker might help the young people to think through:

- the purposes for which they might want to meet
- whether a formal place would actually spoil what they have already
- who they would make representations to, how, when, etc.

This is one way that community work has engaged with children and young people face to face.

Other projects encourage parents, or other concerned adults, to act upon the needs of children. Sometimes this is because the parents also benefit. The development of a pre-school playgroup may indeed benefit the child, but it may also free the carer of the child.

Community workers have to take extra care when the impetus for adults to act comes from the children and young people who are causing a nuisance and interfering with adult needs. In places where children engage in unwelcome behaviour, such as vandalism or being noisy, adults can be led to realise that there is little or no social provision for the children. The result is that the adults organise themselves to provide an adventure playground or a youth group. This is very often successful where it addresses the initial problem of disturbed relationships between adults and children, and community workers often keep this issue on the agenda. On the other hand, there can be empty youth clubs and deserted playgrounds if the provision is developed by adults who set out to distance themselves further from young people rather than to maintain a relationship.

Other projects do not necessarily aim at children and young people but nevertheless involve and benefit them. A post-war council estate included a street where the houses had not been modernised like those in the surrounding streets. Part of the problem was the fact that kitchens and bathrooms were not properly separated, a situation that was seen as basic to the whole family's health.

An action group was formed, meeting in different people's homes, and children could be seen sitting on the floor during the meetings. When negotiations with the housing department became stuck, and the meeting planned its protest at the housing office the following day, children coloured-in protest banners as the adults discussed tactics. When the protest took place there were lots of children present, some in pushchairs, some to swell the numbers, and they helped to give a homely picture to the local press.

During the course of any community project, it may be that all these different approaches are harnessed. Rarely do projects find that complex human relationships fall into tidy parcels.

Children are a significant part of community life. We often hear people say that the time when they have most friends in the neighbourhood is when they have children for whom they have to care. It may even be that children contribute to community life to an extent that far outweighs their numbers.

Those who sponsor projects think of children in different ways. In the past, Sunday schools brought churches in touch with adults – 'working through the children'. Some community projects also think of children as a way of getting to the parents – a means to other objectives. I hope to suggest that children are an integral part of the community though the reality appears to be that most community work projects work with adults even when the objectives are formulated around the needs of children.

Community – the Setting for Children's Growth

Since most community work projects of the neighbourhood type are in disadvantaged communities, they are in what I call working-class communities. However, since the latest fashion appears to be to describe people by their consumption rather than their production potential, I shall refer to these areas as low-income areas.

This issue of power, and how it is understood to work in low-income areas (compared with suburban areas), provides an important part of the backcloth against which children grow up. In low-income areas people seldom have the opportunity to develop their skills, and the pressure on their time and resources is often considerable. That is why community projects are placed in such communities. A major reason why people in these areas are able to engage with a particular issue is that skills, resources and time can be shared. It is this that enables an objective to be pursued. In other words, a number of actors make different contributions to enable something to happen. The 'power to do' depends on different people positioning themselves in relation to one another. The power to do is 'held' between them. So when we describe this as a collective activity, we refer to the strategic positioning of contributors, rather than the mere accumulation of numbers.

In the 'do-it-yourself' culture of suburban Britain power is seen as an independent quality that you either have or not. Power is owned. Christopher Bowler (1992) points out that suburbia is about dreams. The huge pride in civic buildings or large cathedrals once felt by communities is now individualised, and personal dreams are expressed by the do-it-yourself character of people's own houses. This is accompanied by the personal choice to join the golf club or some other community of interest. He suggests that social units are purely functional. He thinks that these dreams are not just materialistic, but that 'the dream of respectability, for example, can generate almost limitless activity to ward off the ghastly spectre of failure'. The 'power to do' is by implication a matter of personal choice, something 'owned'.

Some of these features are present in low-income areas, and what is described here is not an either/or situation. Nevertheless the distinction is clear enough to express how different communities go about organising their activities.

It is interesting that both these concepts of power of being 'held' and being 'owned' – relate to concepts of 'belonging'. The power being held among and between people relates to our belonging to one another, and the power that is personally owned relates to our possessions.

Angus Wood (1987) gives an example of a street where the housing stock is mainly four-bedroomed houses occupied by families with children. As a result, children literally fight for play space. Community fragmentation caused by the hostility between children makes co-operative action difficult for children and adults alike. Past memories of successful community action are clouded by a general feeling that nothing is likely to happen. Community workers may want to use the opportunity of creating play space to evoke the qualities of hope necessary to overcome the inertia of lethargy and despair that block other developments in the community.

The bringing to the foreground those qualities that enliven human relationships needs to go hand in hand with, and is just as important as, provision for physical needs. Perhaps it is worth considering some of the things that give us a sense of common humanity: engaging in conversations and actions that explore the degrees of, and limits to, our freedom, struggling together with the processes of being in love, of friendships and less intimate relationships. These are some of the things which give people a sense of being human. Adults are no different in this respect to the children and young people who will eventually use the play space. The latter will experience the physical sensations of the equipment and the relational rewards and disappointments of their friendships.

Community work methods are able to work with both the issues of 'belonging' (relationships) and the issue of 'becoming' (human development), as well as issues about generating resources. For low-income areas this could almost be a way of defining community development. If community means that we 'belong', then development means that we 'become'. I am assuming that when we discuss 'human development' or 'becoming' we are holding together both personal and corporate growth, in short, our 'becoming human together' (Hasler, 1992). This is one of the strongest reasons for advocating community development methods in these areas.

I am interested to see that in his chapter (Chapter 9) Roger Adams explores the issue of 'neighbourhood' as a place where a child can develop a sense of separation from family and hence a greater sense of personal identity. This does not contradict my own interest in the neighbourhood as a place of belonging. A growing sense of identity provides children with more to 'contribute', and helps add to their sense of belonging. The converse is also true, in that a wider sense of belonging helps them to expand the sense of their own identity.

These issues become particularly focused when we consider the place of children in communities. More than any other human beings, it is children whom we picture as growing and, more and more, becoming who they are. Child development is so noticeable compared with growth at later stages of the life cycle. The life of children growing up is primarily experienced in their communities and families.

Families and Community

While community initiatives in low-income communities are often very successful, this is sometimes in the face of the demands of the family. People do not readily share resources of any kind when they are in short supply. Family networks are of the utmost importance to people's survival. While waiting in the doorway of a Liverpool family centre I heard an older man who had come to collect his grandchild commenting on a younger man who was passing by, 'He's got seven kids, he won't go short of anything when he gets older will he?' He was expressing the community's understanding of its commitment to its kith and kin. This is one of the stronger influences on the way community workers do their jobs in areas where there are several generations living in the surrounding streets or blocks of flats. Children have to learn, like community workers, how to handle the 'family mafias'.

The housing estates where I have been working over the last 19 years have shown through surveys that the longer the estate has been built the more households there are that are likely to have relatives on the same estate. It is noticeable that mother and daughter ties are very strong. This is still true even though Young and Willmott (1962) wrote their study of East London over 30 years ago. So 'family' is something that can extend into a number of households on an estate. It is therefore quite difficult openly to share with others what precious time, money and skills are available to you, when 'the family' feel that they have first call upon it.

Yet the extended family provides a model of organisation that is based on sharing time, skills and resources. I overheard a conversation once between three sisters who had all received gas bills. The women were deciding whose bill they would pay first. By paying at least one bill there would be the facility for cooking meals for all of them if the other two were cut off before the other bills could be paid. These same three sisters were part of the core of an after-school club activity, and the same atmosphere prevailed in discussions about how to resource the activities of the club. So perhaps the survival needs of family and their structures provide a pattern of organisation that is carried over into the community organisation of playschemes, youth clubs, action groups, environmental projects and many others. By contrast, it may be that in suburban areas structures are marked by a visit to ageing relatives and a phone call. There is greater physical distance between kin. Perhaps personal pension schemes and the relative isolation of each housing unit looking after itself gives a different model for events of a community nature.

Children who have aunts and other relatives in houses on the same estate experience families as being more than just what goes on in their home. By comparison, families who are more dispersed naturally experience the family as being predominantly what goes on in their own household. In the former situation, family links between households merge into other community associations. Rival religious affiliations can mean friendly orientation or suspicion to other extended families. I remember a situation in which, when a child who was too young to be admitted to a community activity was sent home, the parent, a Protestant, complained that although the organisers of the activity were Protestants, in determining the age of the child they had taken the word of a Catholic. Perhaps another factor may concern degrees of respectability. All these things play a part in the means by which children learn who is and who is not an acceptable 'friend'. So although families are important they are not the only social force at work in communities.

With family spread across a number of households the child on the street, even when unsupervised, is in many ways more observed than would be the case in other, more isolated, family units. It may be that as the child grows to gain more freedom, this freedom is not appreciated as private behaviour but as the freedom of opportunity that takes place in public view and in a public context – despite the fact we often associate freedom with personal privacy. This experience of socialisation leads us to understand children's growth in opportunity – children's 'becoming' – as taking place in the setting of their 'belonging'.

Community workers have long had an appropriate view of neighbourhood work which has wanted to avoid the kind of parochialism that verges on the sustaining of ghettos. This concern suggests that our 'becoming' can be limited by our 'belonging'. There is no doubt that this danger is ever present. Yet there is another danger. We might see some things as constraints, when they are the very mechanisms that allow power to be held between people, and provide for a public scrutiny that enables greater freedom.

Implications for Community Workers

Before we consider the issue of children's rights I would like to note how this integration of 'belonging' and 'becoming' may affect community work practice.

The first consideration is the way in which community objectives are framed. The present market forces climate sees community objectives as being concerned solely with resources. One sees this in the kind of approach David Thomas (1983) describes as 'smash and grab' community work. Similarly we have the method known as 'community organising', an approach to community action based on the work of Saul Alinsky in the US and currently being applied in several areas in Britain. Here a target to be gained is determined, and flying-picket type activists are bussed in, supposedly to support the local population. The local population is being supported by a few church activists, some of whom do not live in the parish.

This may be a reasonable strategy for change but it is not community work. In the low-income areas I have described it shows no respect for the processes of the community itself. It is tempting to say that it does more to solve the impatient frustrations of community workers than make any difference to the neighbourhood itself. It is put forward as an attempt to create 'becoming' without the support of 'belonging'. Community work is always concerned to approach structural issues, but nothing worthwhile is changed if the objective reached is divorced from the personal change that is brought about and sustained by the presence of the local community.

The second consideration is that work with children is not separable from work with adults. The consequences of work with children have an impact upon adults and vice versa. This is not to say that a project should not aim at a particular age group or category. What often happens is that in their eagerness to be useful people move from solutions to action with very little reflection and analysis. For example, I have heard both local tenants' associations and groups of professionals rush to recommend an adventure playground as a solution to the damage caused by young people. It would be preferable to deploy community workers to explore with young people and adults the nature of the relationship between young people and adults. What kind of contact takes place? Why does each think it happens in the way it does? Upon what concrete evidence are these opinions based?

A danger in our present time is to have too narrow a focus in the way we view work with children. Projects are easily defined in a way that segments the community. Work is often with this group or that management committee, or organised around a single target. An alternative way of defining the work is in relation to the whole, in this case the neighbourhood. To reconsider the situation, mentioned earlier, of children and young people causing damage, a worker may be despatched to help the affected adults to build and manage an adventure playground – seeing the issue through the eyes of the adults, a part. An alternative approach would be to help the community to examine the relationships between the children, young people and adults in the neighbourhood – the whole – and then to help them to form a plan of action together.

The third consideration I would like to examine concerns the ways in which we evaluate community work projects. This issue is intimately connected to the danger of working with the parts rather than the whole and can lead to a very narrow definition of objectives and targets. Short-term involvement in communities is the result, since one stays only until the narrow target is accomplished. This short-term, narrow target style of work is often partly justified on the grounds that it is the kind of work that is easy to understand, and that it has tightly defined boundaries and concrete outputs which will be more likely to attract funding. The implication is that the holistic approach I have suggested leads us into work that is difficult to evaluate.

It is true that if we look at any community as a whole the inter-relationships of people and issues reveal the greater complexity of the way community life is experienced by people who engage in it. As a result good evaluation is particularly welcome because it will enable workers to work with complexity in a systematic way. The problem with the narrower perspective is that it might be seen as a way of getting something done without having to spend money on detailed evaluation. The wider approach opens itself to examine the work on the basis of the 'values' that determine the work. The narrow perspective can too easily allow evaluation to degenerate into nothing more than a cost/benefit exercise. In terms of planning a project we are in danger of allowing targets to be selected not on the strength of the need but on the strength of whether or not they are convenient to evaluate.

These implications are important if we take seriously the idea of children growing up in their communities, and the way that community work can help them to address their hopes and fears.

The Child, the Parent, the Community

When we read what Iona and Peter Opie (1977) say in *The Lore and Language of School Children* we are in no doubt that a child culture exists. The rhymes and games of children and young people are esoteric. In many ways this culture lives on in the street, in the school playground, and in those places where play provision is made by community projects, often run by local people. In many ways this world of play *is* the community of the child.

The child's life is also a life of transition to the culture in which the family is set. Schools provide an academic education that allows a small number of children to escape the more limited opportunities of low-income areas. But teachers are often like community workers – helpful people who do not necessarily provide models that are relevant to the child's background and their social norms. The school 'dinner ladies' may be more useful in this respect. Community activities are often 'driven' by local people who provide models even more useful than the dinner ladies.

The child's aspirations are shaped by a complex interaction, and perhaps contradiction, between local and wider social forces. Yet it is clear that the need for 'belonging' gives the greater weight to family and community influences.

When we set up a community project on the outskirts of Liverpool, some of the issues made clear to us by local people included, 'People like you are always coming round! There's a bit of excitement raised, then we never see you again' and 'The people who live and bring up children round here have a right to the same facilities and chances as anybody else . . . the population deserves to be treated with more respect, somehow.' We were also told that the housing officer would listen to a complaint, write a note on the back of a match box, and then forget about it. The issue of being treated with respect was as high on the agenda as the right to facilities and resources. Children's hopes are shaped by these experiences. Parent's hopes have often taken a beating, but at least one can hope for one's children.

Perhaps the interweaving of the lives of the child, family and community is most evident when we look at where responsibility is seen to lie. In places where children or young people have been suspected or found guilty of killing people, such as the James Bulger case in Liverpool, whole extended families have been harassed to the extent that they have had to leave their homes. It would seem that the community at large, or at least significant sections of it, believes that responsibility belongs not only to the accused but also to their extended families. On the other hand it has also been suggested that this kind of reaction is prompted by a kind of community guilt for not having intervened earlier in such situations. If our understanding of responsibility is a mixture of personal, family and community responses this will probably indicate something about our attitude to rights, as responsibilities and rights tend to go hand in hand.

Community and Children's Rights

First, rights are not the best or only way of improving the situation. There are certain needs which cannot be specified in the language of political and social rights. People sense that they have a right to certain facilities. Some of these can be defined in ways that are enforceable. People sense that they have a right to be treated with respect by their fellow human beings. This does not sound like a right that is enforceable. We may feel that we should have a right of access to certain places and meetings, but it would be impossible to enforce a right to belong.

Michael Ignatieff points out that we are more than 'right bearing' animals. We have other needs that are no less important for our humanity, but which do not find their place easily within the language of constitutional law. He goes on to say:

> It is because fraternity, love, belonging, dignity and respect cannot be specified as rights that we ought to specify them as needs and seek, with the blunt institutional procedures at our disposal, to make their satisfaction a routine human practice. (Ignatieff, 1990, pp. 13–14)

Community development is centrally concerned with these fundamental human needs and their satisfaction, and can be recommended as a method that can engage our humanity within the otherwise cold mechanism of welfare distribution.

It is noticeable that the UN Convention on the Rights of the Child is not a legal document in the sense that its Articles have any status in law. The United Kingdom ratified the Convention as a way of agreeing to its aspirations in order to work towards them. In some ways, given the complexity of community life, community workers might find its underlying principles more a challenge to their practice than the Articles themselves. These are specified by the Children's Rights Development Unit as participation, provision and protection.

In terms of the child's freedom to belong, the principle of participation is based on the concept of the child as an active and contributing participant in society and not merely as a passive recipient of good or bad treatment. I have already commented on the danger of community workers using children as a means of getting at the adults rather than as people in their own right.

The principle of provision covers the rights to survive and develop. These range across the spectrum of physical, mental and spiritual needs, but it is interesting that the Children's Rights Development Unit comments, under this heading, that 'The Convention is clear that the best place for a child is with its parents ...' In other words, it is recognised that the issue of the freedom to 'become' (human development) is interwoven with the freedom to 'belong' (in this case to the family).

Yet some of these issues are within the arena of social and political rights. The right to facilities and opportunities is clearly an example. Our welfare services are regulated, if not funded, by the legislating government. But in the light of the description of the child growing up in community, and the interwoven character of the nexus of relationships between child, family and community, it must remain an open question as to which rights should be the rights of the child, which the rights of the parent and which the rights of the community. The Convention says, too, that the state, in protecting the child, should take into account 'the rights and duties of his or her parents . . . '. It does not suggest that the child's rights are always paramount.

There is a clear challenge to community work to look more closely for opportunities to work directly with children and young people and to listen to their 'voice'. The challenge is to see children and young people as part of the community in their own right. Kath Heaton and Jenny Sayer (1992) have gathered together some useful examples for community workers, noting the ways in which community development has an impact on child welfare. It is important that we hold this growing concern for children's rights within the context of both their communities and their families, extended as they may be across the community. For, as children grow they need the freedom to 'belong' as well as the freedom to 'become'.

Returning to the question posed at the beginning of the chapter, I am aware that I have come down in favour of a needs approach to working with children as opposed to the child's right to choose. This reflects my community work experience and the values which I hope inform my practice. I believe that the search for children-led activities in neighbourhoods has to take place within an awareness of the complex ties between children and adults, particularly in low-income areas. This is the context in which I believe community workers and local people should engage with the issue of children's rights and with the opportunities presented by the Children Act 1989 and the UN Convention.

References

Bowler, C. (1992) 'Faith in Suburbia', unpublished paper.

Hasler, J. (1992) *Becoming Human Together*, Diocese of Bristol, Association of Priority Area Parishes.

Heaton, K. and Sayer, J. (1992) *Community Development and Child Welfare*, London: CDF/The Children's Society.

Ignatieff, M. (1990) *The Needs of Strangers*, London: Hogarth Press.

Opie, I. and P. (1977) *The Lore and Language of School Children*, London: Granada Publishing.

Thomas, D. (1983) *The Making of Community Work*, London: George Allen & Unwin.

Wood, A. (1987) 'Pilgrimage in Practice' unpublished paper.

Young, M. and Willmott, P. (1962) *Family and Kinship in East London*, revised edition, Harmondsworth: Penguin Books.

Conclusion: Rights, Participation and Neighbourhoods

Peter Newell

Make no mistake, as a society our sentimentality over children runs little more than skin-deep. The tide of feeling for and against children ebbs and flows in society at large, just as it does in individual communities and individual families. In the UK it has seemed at times as if we were living through a sustained wave of primitive hatred of children, and a widespread scapegoating of children for adult-caused problems. An isolated, almost unique, tragedy in 1993 – the vicious murder of a Liverpool two year old, James Bulger, by two ten year olds – provoked an outpouring of deep-rooted adult suspicions, fears and venom: the *Lord of the Flies* nightmare, the doctrine of original sin, a construction of children who 'had the faces of normal boys but hearts of unparalleled evil' (*Daily Mirror*, 1993).

If we were a child-friendly society we really would have relegated the idea of original sin to fiction. We would accept that children are far, far more sinned against than sinning, and that almost invariably their sinning has direct roots in adult apathy or active cruelty. We would be filled with horror by the tragedy of James Bulger's death, but it would release a new energy to do better to protect all children from the adult-caused poverty, instability and violence-breeding-violence that exists in so many 'communities'.

Instead, we put James's two diminutive murderers through the charade of an 'adult' criminal trial which established beyond reasonable doubt their guilt for his killing, but made no attempt to establish why. There is then an automatic 'indefinite' sentence, locking up two 11 year olds to be detained, in the give-away penal language, 'during Her Majesty's pleasure'.

Riding on the tide of public and/or media feeling, the Home Secretary enthusiastically announced new plans to lock up more and younger children for longer periods. Everybody he asked – and a lot of organisations and people he did not ask – told him it would not work. It would make the children and the problem worse not better. But that was not the point. The point was to be seen to be doing something, and imprisoning more young children, even in the last years of the twentieth century, satisfies majority adult instincts. We saw those raw instincts in the mobs which tried to attack the big vans taking the two accused children to and from court. If as a society we loved and respected children, we could not contemplate locking up 11-year-olds indefinitely, or locking them up at all unless doing so was thought to be the only way of containing an immediate, serious and continuing threat to others (we know that murderers of any age seldom pose such a threat).

There was another sobering, relevant and lasting image of the Bulger tragedy: the many adult witnesses of James's last walk with his murderers, none of whom intervened, grotesquely symbolised the ability of communities to note but not intervene in the daily suffering of children. The intensity of the media coverage meant that most of us must have asked ourselves what we would have done; would we have been any more interventionist, any more effective in averting the tragedy? Would we? Why not?

Children, you might think, are the obvious priority on any progressive political agenda. As the preceding chapters show, they are the future: concern for children, linked to concern for the environment, are the crucial elements in any future planning, whether for a neighbourhood, a local community, a nation or the community of nations. Over the last few decades we have become scientifically aware of the damage humans have done to their environment, of how near to oblivion disregard for it has led us. With children too, there is increasing understanding of the level of adult harm and abuse of children within every society and of its influence on the depravity and violence of succeeding generations of adults.

First Call for Children

The World Summit for Children in New York in 1990 was the largest meeting of heads of government the world has ever seen

– 71 presidents or prime ministers from 159 nations. The summit promoted a fundamental principle:

> That the lives and normal development of children should have first call on society's concerns and capacities and that children should be able to depend on that commitment in good times and in bad, in normal times and times of emergency, in times of peace and in times of war, in times of prosperity and in times of recession.

Marking the third anniversary of the Summit in September 1993, the UN Secretary-General reported that the Summit had produced 'a global consensus not only on principles, but also on strategy. Now we must work on tactics'. Of all the subjects of development,

> none has the acceptance, or the power, to mobilize, as does the cause of children. Our children are our future . . . There is universal acceptance that investment in children is an investment in the future of humanity. It is essential to social development. It contributes to economic prosperity. It sustains families and promotes gender equality. And it provides a foundation for lasting peace and democracy.

These high-minded sentiments have as much relevance and truth at community level as they do at a global level. But at no level as yet has there been much progress to translate the words into active policies. We are barely yet in a position to envisage what societies and communities dedicated to the principle of first call for children would look like. But it is surely important to try, and an attempt, however crude, seems an appropriate conclusion to this book.

If we cannot get priorities right at the basic level of individual families (used in the widest sense to refer to the adults – one, two or several – most immediately responsible for the child) we are unlikely to get it right in neighbourhoods, or communities or society at large. So for a start in a child-centred society we would make a big and serious thing out of preparing for parenthood. Discussion of it, of family life education would not be edged out of or marginalised within the school curriculum the way it is. Nor incidentally would education law allow parents to remove their children from school sex education, or school governors to decide not to provide sex education. These legal provisions, added in the last few years, illustrate how bigoted and untrusting adult attitudes have been allowed to undermine children's rights to a basic form of preparation for adult life and for responsible parenthood.

Birth would be a cause for a lot more obvious celebration than it generally is today. For those who remain active members of religious faiths there are naming ceremonies of various kinds but their significance has if anything lessened. The legal obligation to register a birth, the formal recording of the name of the new person, is at the moment a tiresome formality taking place generally in cold and bureaucratic surroundings. But it could become the moment for symbolic and formal recognition of the significance of parental responsibility for the child's welfare, and of wider family and community responsibility for the child, a time for celebrations and parties. A start has been made over this: plans to support those who wish to make more of naming ceremonies, and formalise the assumption of parental and wider responsibilities for new children are currently being developed by Lord Young of Dartington and others.

Parental Responsibility

There has already been some recognition that parents do not 'own' their children, or have absolute rights over them. The House of Lords judgment in 1986 on the celebrated 'Gillick' case emphasised that the rights parents have over children are not absolute, but are for the promotion of the welfare of the child. The concept of parental 'responsibility' appears in the Children Act 1989, but it is not developed: the definition is circular and unhelpful – 'all the rights, duties, powers, responsibilities and authority which by law a parent of a child has in relation to the child and his property' (Children Act 1989, section 3). The Scottish Law Commission, in its 1992 proposals for reform of family law, proposes a more expanded statement, including responsibilities 'to safeguard and promote the child's health, development and welfare, and to provide, in a manner appropriate to the child's stage of development, direction and guidance to the child' (Scottish Law Commission, 1992).

Other countries have gone very much further than the UK towards setting out basic principles for childrearing and child care in their family law. In Finland, for example, a 1983 Act states:

The objects of custody are to ensure the well-being and the well-balanced development of a child according to his individual needs and wishes, and to ensure for a child close and affectionate human relationships in particular between a child and his parents.

A child shall be ensured good care and upbringing as well as the supervision and protection appropriate to his age and stage of development. A child should be brought up in a secure and stimulating environment and should receive an education that corresponds to his wishes, inclinations and talents.

A child shall be brought up in the spirit of understanding, security and love. He shall not be subdued, corporally punished or otherwise humiliated. His growth towards independence, responsibility and adulthood shall be encouraged, supported and assisted.

The Act goes on to give 'custodians' duties to safeguard the child's development and well-being according to these provisions (Child Custody and Right of Access Act 1983, section 1).

If we accept the principle of first call for children we need a legal framework that sets out such principles; the continuing absence of one inhibits children's growth, and the growth of healthy communities and a society which respects children's welfare and rights. We cannot leave it to chance, to the whims of individual adults, because far too many adults still perceive children as property, sometimes as objects of concern, but seldom as individual people with views and feelings of their own.

The Child's Voice

Respect for the views and feelings of individual children and groups of children would be reflected in the law, and demonstrated in policy and practice at every level. Legal obligations to consult children and take their views seriously would apply within the family – to all those with parental responsibility. The Scottish Law Commission report referred to above proposed that anyone exercising parental responsibility and taking a major decision which relates to a child should 'ascertain the views of the child regarding the decision and give due consideration to them, having regard to the child's age and maturity' (p. 18). In other countries such obligations are already reflected in the law: in Finland, the Act quoted above goes on to require 'custodians' of children, before making a decision to 'discuss the matter with the child, taking into account the child's age and maturity and the nature of the matter. In making the decision the custodian shall give due consideration to the child's feelings, opinions and wishes' (section 4).

Of course such laws are not in any normal sense enforceable. But, as the Scottish Law Commission argued:

> it emphasises that the child is a person in his or her own right and that his or her views are entitled to respect and consideration . . . There could be value in a provision which established a duty to consult the child, even if it was vague and unenforceable. It could have an influence on behaviour.

Beyond the family, the education system would be built on the principle of active participation by children, with education law providing formal rights. Children as well as parents and community interests would influence school choice. Within schools children would be perceived as active participants in learning from the moment they walked or crawled in the door, not as empty vessels to be filled with a diet dictated in detail by a distant Secretary of State. School rules would be the rules of the community, addressed equally to adults and to children. Chapter 7 illustrates just how far Ministers are from recognising that education is about increasing control over one's own life, and that it will not happen in school communities that remain generally authoritarian, hierarchical and undemocratic. The chapter also shows that exciting examples of active involvement and participation in schooling happen despite rather than because of the law (and artificial barriers between school and community do get broken down, as Rupert Prime describes in Chapter 6). There is not a single provision in the thousands of sections of current Education Acts which promotes the child's voice.

In the health service there is at least more of a debate on children's rights to consent and withhold consent to treatment. In a child-centred society, children from as early as possible would be seen as active participants in their own health care, having, from the moment that they expressed a desire, access to their own health records, registered with their own GP and dentist.

They would also be seen as the individual clients of social services, with separate files, separate rights of confidentiality, and unqualified rights to attend case conferences and other meetings at which significant decisions may be made about their lives. Here again, as the chapters in Part I indicate, there has been some progress. Our Children Act obliges local authorities 'looking after' children, some other institutions and certain courts hearing certain sorts of cases to listen to children's views and take them seriously.

It is interesting that adult suspicions and fears often misinterpret modest advocacy of children's right to participate in decision making as a liberationist proposal that children should alone make decisions. A lot of the criticism of the modest advances for children's rights made by the Children Act is based on this sort of misrepresentation.

Children in Government

In local government right down through the levels of parish councils and neighbourhood and community committees there would be representation of children's views and interests through elected representatives and advisory councils, through child impact statements prepared on all policy options that may affect children. These arrangements would need to ensure representation which reflects the interests of particular groups of children by race, gender and disability. It must not be forgotten that some children will be unable through extreme youth or extreme disability to express views, and there must be arrangements for careful consideration and advocacy of their interests too. As Jim Radford argues in his chapter, there are the beginnings of representation of 'youth' interests in some areas, through youth councils, but often the age group involved has more in common with adult interests than with children's. There could be local children's rights commissioners empowered to promote children's needs and rights and ensure that their voice is heard and taken seriously, and to represent directly the interests of those unable to represent themselves.

There would be a proliferation of organisations of children, both local and national, organisations like the National Association of Young People in Care, Black and in Care (see Chapter 2), and the National Union of School Students. They would be supported and funded by government, respected, consulted and quoted in local and national debates.

At central government level . . . well, certainly the voting age would be lowered below 18 (if you can marry, and fight for your country at 16, why can't you vote?). In Nicaragua and Brazil 16-year-olds have the vote now. And why at 16? If children were able to register to vote from the moment they could demonstrate alone to a registrar that they understood the purpose and the procedure, they would have earned their vote by passing a test which many current 'adult' voters would undoubtedly fail (in fact there is no logic in making them, or them alone, take a test – the idea is the product of a condescending adult mind). The age at which you can stand to be a member of Parliament or a councillor would also come tumbling down below 21.

And there would be a statutory office or offices to represent children's rights and interests at government level, to seek to ensure that they had means of redress when their rights were breached, and more child-impact statements. Positive models exist in other countries: Norway established the post of Barneombud, the world's first children's ombudsman, in 1981; in New Zealand there is a statutory Commissioner for Children and in South Australia the Children's Interests Bureau. These have become respected, influential and popular institutions. In Norway an opinion poll in 1989 found that 83 per cent of Norwegians believed the office should continue (Flekkoy, 1991).

In the UK a detailed feasibility study for the appointment of a statutory children's rights commissioner was published in 1991; more than 50 major organisations, including four royal colleges of health, now support the campaign for a commissioner, and the Labour Party included the proposal, together with that for a minister for children, in its manifesto for the 1992 general election (Rosenbaum and Newell, 1991).

Child Friendly Policies

What sort of policies would emerge in society and in local communities, once the legal framework was in place, and children's views and interests were adequately represented and considered?

Once such principles are established it follows that the state must be respectful of every new baby's immediate need for a very close and continuous relationship with at least one key adult. Child care must be cherished and rewarded as the most important occupation in the world. Penelope Leach sets out in detail some of the implications, writing as an angry advocate for children in western societies which 'have left little time or space for children and no easy way for adults to be both solvent self-respecting citizens and caring parents' (Leach, 1994).

Employment law would be reframed to allow for proper periods of parental leave, for flexible working and work sharing between parents. The UK would no longer be exposed as the anti-child voice in the European Union, isolated in blocking implementation of the modest standards of the European Directive on Parental Leave. The world of work would look very different very quickly, technology being harnessed to enable many more to work from their homes, and thus give their growing children more time and more attention (recent research suggests that over a single generation the amount of time parents spend with their children may have reduced by as much as 40 per cent). Workplace nurseries, where they mean commuting journeys for babies and little real contact with parents, may be a convenience for employers but are not a positive option for children.

Advertisements would illustrate the wide variety of job sharing and flexitime on offer; employers would be competing to provide the most child-friendly contracts, and child-friendly premises. Wherever possible, the workplace would itself be welcoming to even very young children (and all workplaces should open to children and be prepared to explain and justify their role and functions to children). While hopefully a new-found child-focused altruism would be the main motivator, there would be clear financial incentives too.

All those working in and for the community would have a common purpose of seeking to minimise the isolation that can come from lone caring for babies and young children. Some family centres, some community centres, toy libraries and schools achieve this for some carers and children, providing a place to meet, to talk, to share information, achievements and problems. Chapter 1 outlines the potential of the family centre to grow into a self-run, self-help group. But all too often because of their rarity such places are perceived as stigmatising – for 'problem' families, 'at risk' children. Every community needs such a place, a children's place, an 'ordinary' focus, filled with sufficient useful amenities to make it attractive to all parents and carers at one time or another. In the home, essential safety equipment – stair gates, fireguards and so on – would be available through loan systems or necessary subsidy as a protective right of the child.

Only in the most extreme situations in which the child's best interests genuinely justified it would children be separated from their key adults. The alienating experiences described by Kanchan Jadeja in Chapter 2, and the potential offered by respecting community values, have profound implications. As a matter of course, criminal courts would consider the parenting responsibilities of those convicted before sentencing. We would no longer read of the tragedy of families divided by deportation. The 'public' interest, the interests of the criminal justice system or of immigration control, would be subservient to children's rights to continuity of parenting.

Challenging Inequality

Placing such a clear priority on children's welfare, all children's welfare, would not tolerate the extremes of inequality of our present society. We look back now on a decade in which the proportion of children living in poverty in the UK has trebled from 10 to 31 per cent. The definition of poverty is that accepted across Europe – families living on less than half average income. The number of children living in families dependent on basic benefit also more than trebled between 1979 and 1992. The real income of the poorest 10 per cent shows a significant fall, while there has been a rise of 36 per cent for the average. Poverty, as the Archbishop of Canterbury's *Faith in the City* report concluded in 1985, is not just about a shortage of money: 'It is about rights and relationships; about how people are treated and how they regard themselves; about powerlessness, exclusion and loss of dignity . . . ' Craig Russell's Chapter 8 illustrates the neighbourhood dimensions of destructive inequality and poverty.

If the focus was on the child victims, and on the imperative of their growth and development for our growth and development as a worthwhile society, then any sign of escalating child poverty, of homeless children or children dumped with families in bare and dangerous bed and breakfast rooms or hostels would be quickly challenged by redistributive policies; by, for example, supporting rather than scapegoating single parents and targeting more benefits on children.

And the necessary information on which to make judgements about 'adequate' standards of living, about the impact of policies and changes in policy on children, would be readily available, not deliberately clouded by statistical sleight of hand.

Similarly with changes in basic services like the health service. There would be no question of suddenly discovering, as we are now, that children are dying because of a lack of specialist paediatric care in many areas (British Paediatric Association, 1993). Instead, before any significant changes in organisation and delivery of health services, their potential effects on sensitive indicators of child health would have been carefully weighed up. Children would not of course be the only group whose needs are carefully considered. But there could be no question of suddenly acknowledging a worsening of services to some children. Market forces would never be permitted to challenge children's health rights.

Environment Fit for Children

All of us would be more respectful of children's health needs, giving a new priority to environmental issues, like reducing air and water pollution, cleaning up dirty beaches and seeking to stop ozone depletion, ending tobacco advertising, because all these things affect the developing minds and bodies of children more seriously than they do those of adults. In December 1993 the government, with ministerial glee, forced the European Union to slow down the clean-up of dirty beaches, and adopt less stringent conditions for tap water. It is predominantly children's health, and in some cases children's lives, which are threatened by a wide range of adult-caused environmental hazards. Yet children's interests were not considered when Euro-politicians bartered to delay removing poisonous lead from our water supply, raw sewage from our beaches. There is strong evidence that air pollution, mostly from cars, is responsible for a sharp increase in asthma among children.

Priority concern for children would lead in time to their regaining their mobility in neighbourhoods and communities. Transport and planning policies would be radically altered by consideration of children's interests. Cars would lose their right of way in many areas; there would be a reversal of policies which have encouraged them in ever-increasing numbers to belch out pollution at child-level, and to criss-cross children's territory. The chapters in Part 2 show how children's involvement, on a small or large scale, can already transform neighbourhoods in the direction of their needs.

Also relevant to mobility, the inter-generational paranoia about on the one hand 'stranger-danger' to children and on the other young muggers threatening the elderly would be replaced by a realistic understanding of the true scale of such violence, and of the community strategies that we know already can reduce it. Thus children's (and everyone else's) safe neighbourhood would expand so that they could walk and run, and bicycle to and from school. Children would appear again playing alone in streets and parks. The right to safe play, argued for by Roger Adams in Chapter 9, would be restored. Talking to children would not be seen as the prelude to abusive behaviour, and crossing the street to intervene to help distressed children would be expected and welcomed.

Every child would have easy access by foot or bike to common areas where the restrictions were not on their mobility but on that of adults and dogs – yes, dogs' freedom to excrete where they wish would be curtailed for the sake of children's freedom to play safely – what a challenge to national priorities!

Public transport would become friendly to children and to carers – safe, cheap, accessible and interesting (playrooms on long-distance trains). The built environment would be welcoming to children, with doors that they can open safely, handles on their level, child-sized furniture and windows at their height. Public places, restaurants and shops would compete over the warmth of welcome offered to children and their carers. And when carer and child were having a bad time together (tantrums would still happen in super-markets now and then, however far competing stores went to make shopping an attractive experience for children and their carers) the looks and gestures from others would be of constructive sympathy, followed up with offers of help and distraction.

Schools would in time look and certainly feel very different (although it is schools, one suspects, that will be most resistant to real change). They too would be operating flexitime, would not keep children standing out in the cold at adult convenience until some magic bell allows them in to 'their' school, nor herd them all out for lengthy periods in mid morning and lunch. Given the inflexible, standard model of schooling that has developed, it is much more difficult to predict what institutional forms would truly reflect freedom of education for children, but quite easy to know what features have no place in it: regimented classes, compulsory uniforms, externally imposed detailed curricula, etc.

An early legislative step would be quickly to remove, with some embarrassment, the unique rights which adults have to hit and humiliate children. When it comes to children, the law on assault draws its protective circle not around the child but around the punishing parent or other adult. Physical punishment of children in the home is the only form of interpersonal violence which remains socially and legally acceptable in our society – a highly symbolic sign of the low status of children. Coupled with legal reform would be a high-profile and comprehensive information campaign on positive childrearing, caring and education without violence or humiliation. Within a generation one could hope for non-violent conflict resolution to be established as the only respectable way of resolving problems whether within the family, the neighbourhood, the community, the nation or between potentially warring nations. Punitive and vengeful attitudes, backing punitive and vengeful criminal justice systems and institutions, born out of childhood experiences of adult cruelty and revenge, would be replaced with policies which see rehabilitation and necessary reparation as their only aims.

On the media, children would not only receive a fair share of programming for their interests and leisure, carefully researched. Their news would feature in news programmes, their views would be featured in current affairs and political discussions. The effects of new policies, new laws and new developments on children would be reported as keenly as effects on other age groups. The concept of equal opportunities for children and young people to participate in the arts and culture would begin to make an impact on distribution of resources for youth arts. (The National Playing Fields Association has estimated that the Department of National Heritage spends 3p on the needs of children for every £100 spent on adult leisure.)

Finally, it may be a more painful exercise to look closer to home, even at home: how different would your relationships with children you may live or work with, your working life be, reorganised along the lines of first call for children? Take the principle of participation. Most of us probably ask our children's views on some issues . . . but how often and how consistently, and how seriously do we take their responses? How much have we modified our lives and our behaviour to fit with our children's needs and rights? And how much have they had to modify to fit in with ours?

The UN Convention

In several chapters of this book the United Nations Convention on the Rights of the Child has been quoted. A lot of hope is being invested in the power of the Convention as an international instrument to ensure that the world's good intentions towards children lead to action, to better lives for children. The Convention, in over 40 substantive articles, provides principles and detailed standards to test our government's and our own treatment of children. By 1994 over 150 countries worldwide had ratified – fully accepted – the Convention. If its principles and standards are taken seriously they can only lead towards the sort of child-centred societies and communities outlined above. In fact one article or another if fully implemented would guarantee to all children all the developments outlined above, and many more. Article 12, for example, guarantees children the right to express their views freely and have them given due weight, and in particular the right to be heard in any administrative or judicial proceedings which affect them. It is coupled with rights of freedom of expression, thought, conscience and religion; freedom of association and protection of privacy. Article 3 upholds the best interests of the child as a primary consideration in all actions concerning them. Article 2 insists on equal rights for all children without discrimination of any kind, and other articles emphasise the rights of particular groups – disabled children, refugee and adopted children, children without families and children of minorities. Article 19 underlines the child's right to physical and personal integrity, to protection from 'all forms of physical or mental violence'.

Given the worldwide remit of the Convention, social and economic rights are outlined with less preciseness . . . an 'adequate' standard of living, the right to 'benefit from social security', an obligation to ensure 'to the maximum extent possible' the survival and development of the child. But interpreted with good intentions, such provisions combine with absolute civil and political rights to provide a framework for building child-centred nations and communities.

In the UK there is no serious sign of good intentions. The government, which ratified the Convention in December 1991, has so far expended a tiny proportion of the time of two officials in a corner of the giant Department of Health on the task of implementation and reporting to the UN Committee on the Rights of the Child. Countries which ratify have to report in detail on progress towards implementation two years after ratification and then every five years. The UK's first report, published in 1994, was a deeply complacent document, dishonest by omission and providing no recognisable picture of the state of our children.

When it is challenged on its record affecting children, on the lack of serious implementation of the Convention, or on the need for a governmental office to represent children's rights and needs (the proposal for a children's rights commissioner), the response is always the same – that the Children Act 1989 does all that is needed for children. The response has fooled a lot of people. The reality is that the Children Act is a major reform of aspects of children's law. But it is not by any stretch of the imagination a charter of children's rights. It affects limited numbers of children, certain services for children (in particular child care, child protection and daycare) and certain court hearings. It contains no over-arching principles to dictate communities' or even parents' attitudes to children.

The Children Act is a staging post on the way towards legislation that comprehensively reflects the principles of the Convention. Its significance for children's rights has been vastly exaggerated. Partly because of that, the advances it does make are now under attack.

Of course, even in the UK, it is possible to be optimistic. Children's rights have become respectable; major reports have promoted 'the child as a person not an object of concern' and have acknowledged that we have only now begun to expose the tip of the iceberg of adult cruelty to children; organisations dedicated to the development of children's legal rights have emerged and gained influence; all the major children's organisations have 'adopted' the Convention and begun to take participation by children and young people seriously, and all support the proposal for a statutory children's rights commissioner; within a scattering of local authorities children's rights officers have been appointed to advocate children's views and interests and take up their complaints; and new and detailed charters have built on the framework of the Convention – charters for play, charters for children in hospital, in care . . .

Until children's rights are given reality in the home, and in neighbourhoods and communities through local action, they remain abstract. And rights are not just attached to individual children – the Convention implies collective and community rights. Moving on from where we are now demands mechanisms for moving from the abstract into practice, and schools, projects and local initiatives can provide many of them.

The potential to be derived from bringing together the rights agenda for children and community development is enormous.

We will need to go on arguing the case for children's rights, but also indicate with growing confidence and a growing range of positive examples how the rights can be given meaning. Action at neighbourhood level with and by children must be part of the overall strategy. That is why this book is important: not many examples of children-led activities, but plenty of material hinting at the way forward!

So far most of this progress is paper progress, words on paper. More optimism would come from more practical examples of progress in communities, of children making the running in their neighbourhood, their community, and of the community of children making a clear impact on national life. Such examples would have made a better book. But that few such examples exist does not diminish our individual responsibility. On the contrary, the message is clear enough. There are more than enough words to point us in the right direction. It is up to us to enable children to adopt the status they deserve as people within the family, the neighbourhood, communities and the nation.

You can start now, and you can be sure it will change the quality of your life too . . .

References

British Paediatric Association (1993) *The Care of Critically Ill Children*, statement, 24 November.

Daily Mirror, 25 November 1993.

Flekkoy, M.G. (1991) *A Voice for Children*, London: Jessica Kingsley.

Leach, P. (1994) *Children First*, London: Michael Joseph.

Rosenbaum, M. and Newell, P. (1991) *Taking Children Seriously: A Proposal for a Children's Rights Commissioner*, London: Gulbenkian Foundation.

Scottish Law Commission (1992) *Report on Family Law*, Edinburgh: HMSO, p. 3.

Index